The statute of limitations in New York State is one of the most restrictive in all of America and many good people are working hard to change the current law which denies justice for survivors. I hope that Stephen Fife's eloquent first-person account will help the public understand the life-long consequences of child sexual abuse and put a spotlight on the need to hold institutions accountable for exposing and preventing it.

    —Assemblywoman Margaret M. Markey
      • Sponsor of the Child Victims Act of New York

The 13th Boy is a harrowing glimpse into the psychological process of grooming a teenager for sexual abuse. Fife's courageous telling of his personal story while a student at Horace Mann sheds light on a subject too long kept in the dark.

    —Amos Kamil
      • "Prep School Predators"
      New York Times Magazine
      • Co-author of "Great Is The Truth: the Secret History
      of Sexual Abuse at the Horace Mann School"

The 13th Boy is spot on, edgy, funny, insightful, and empathy-inspiring! With sharp wit and harrowing detail, in a voice true to teen experience, Steve Fife chronicles his psychological abduction by his revered mentor. I was reading at 5:00 AM until my Kindle fell out of my hands.

    —Mindy Lewis
      • Author of *Life Inside: A Memoir*

Abuse is too often presented as a crime that assaults its victims with sudden and searing violence. Steve Fife's rigorously honest portrait of the abuse that teachers visited upon teenagers at Horace Mann School in New York explores the much more troubling and insidious nature of abuse by teachers— how a gifted teacher can be at once intellectually and emotionally alluring, yet also so controlling and manipulative as to sap the soul.

    —Marc Fisher
      • Senior Editor at the *Washington Post*
      • Author of a *New Yorker* article on abuse at Horace Mann

Read this book! Steve Fife's courageous and vivid recounting of these painful experiences will help you to understand what it is like to go through this. If you know someone who was abused, please read this book and understand their experience. If you yourself were abused, then read this book and know that you are NOT ALONE.

    ——Joseph Cumming
      • Pastor of the International Church at Yale University
      • Founder of the Horace Mann Survivors "Not Alone" group

The 13th Boy

Dedication
For my Mom, in good times and bad.

Here we are with our finite beings and physical senses
in the presence of a universe whose possibilities are infinite.
— Alfred North Whitehead

For the infinite air is unkind.
— Gerard Manley Hopkins

The 13th Boy

A Memoir of Education & Abuse

Stephen Fife

Cune

The 13th Boy:
A Memoir of Education and Abuse
© 2015 Stephen Fife
Cune Press, Seattle 2015
First Edition
2 4 6 8 9 7 5 3
Hardback ISBN 9781614571124 $34.95
Paperback ISBN 9781614571131 $19.95
eBook ISBN 9781614571148 $9.99
Kindle ISBN 9781614571155 $9.99
Credits
Back Cover Photos of Horace Mann by Peter Brooks
Author photo pg 196 by Dan Winters
Cover Design by Gary Albright

A Note to the Reader

The names of classmates and friends in this book are pseudonyms, unless otherwise specified. The names of the teachers are real. Also, all the quotes from famous writers that appear in this book have been taken from my high school notebooks and have been transcribed exactly as I recorded them there. Finally, the poems that appear are substantially the same as I wrote them way back when.

Resources

For practical help with the problem of abuse in education, please see the Resources section on page 188. In addition to the brief Bibliography listed here, we are providing online a more detailed list of websites, articles, and books, that were compiled by Peter Brooks as well as additional supporting material. See: www.cunepress.com/ttb

TABLE OF CONTENTS

Introduction 9

PART ONE

Chapter 1   12

Chapter 2   17

Chapter 3   23

Chapter 4   27

Chapter 5   34

Chapter 6   42

Chapter 7   46

Chapter 8   55

Chapter 9   60

Chapter 10   64

Chapter 11   74

Chapter 12   79

PART TWO

Chapter 1   86

Chapter 2   94

Chapter 3   99

Chapter 4   105

Chapter 5   110

Chapter 6   116

Chapter 7   120

Chapter 8   126

Chapter 9   132

Chapter 10   138

Chapter 11   141

Chapter 12   150

Chapter 13   157

Chapter 14   164

Epilogue   179

RESOURCES

How To Protect Your Child   188

Bibliography:
Books & Articles on Abuse   192

Acknowledgements   194

Index   195

Author's Bio   196

The Member of the Group

OCTOBER 13, 2012 WAS A BEAUTIFUL day to be in New York City. And if you were lucky enough to be there on that Saturday, then there was no more beautiful part of the city to be in than the Battery Park City promenade facing the Hudson River. The sun was shining, the sky was a cloudless azure-blue, the aqua-green water sparkled; runners ran gracefully, mothers pushed strollers effortlessly, couples strolled along the walkway or leaned on the railing watching the boats wend their way downriver. There was a timeless quality to the afternoon, a sense of lazy elegance, as if hunger and poverty and all the pressing problems of the world had been banished to some metaphysical back burner, so as not to interfere with the perfect harmony of the day.

I was there too, sitting on a green bench facing the water, admiring the scenery and trying not to think about why I was here. Finally I grew tired of having no one to share this with and called up an ex-girlfriend in Pasadena, a college professor.

"It's so beautiful here right now," I told her. "It's moments like these that make me really regret not living here anymore."

"Right, and what are rents like down there?" she reminded me. "Like $7,000 a month for a tiny one bedroom?"

"Yeah, well, a person can dream, can't he?" I sighed.

"What are you doing back in New York anyway? Is one of your plays being done there?" she asked.

"I wish," I said. Then there was a pause, a long one, as I realized that I was going to have to describe what I had been trying so hard not to think about.

"Steve? Are you still there?" she asked.

"Remember that teacher I told you about when we first started going out? The one from my high school?"

"The really twisted one?"

"Yeah."

"He committed suicide, right?"

"If only," I said with a clipped laugh. "No, someone else committed suicide. This guy is still very much alive."

"And you're going to see him? To tell him how you feel?"

That sounded nice when she said it, so simple and straightforward. Two people in a room, I turn to him and say, "Here are my feelings about what you did to me." Or no. "Here are my feelings about what happened between us." And then he would turn to me and—the fantasy just broke apart. Words failed. Because there are some people who you simply have nothing more to say to; and who have nothing more to say to you. Not in this lifetime. Or in several lifetimes to come, if that's how it works.

"No. I'm part of a group now," I told her. "We're having a meeting here."

"What kind of a group?"

"We all went to the same high school."

"And you were all messed with by the same teacher?" she asked.

"Well, yes and no," I told her. "There are a few others in the group who had been 'messed with' by that same teacher. But most of the people in the group have been 'messed with' by other teachers at the school."

"How many people in the group?" she asked.

"Around thirty," I said.

"And how many teachers who did this?"

"At least fifteen. Maybe more."

"What?" she screamed into the phone, so I had to hold it away from my ear. "Fifteen teachers messing with students at the same high school at the same time? How is that even possible?"

"It didn't all happen at the same time," I said. "It happened over a period of years. Twenty-five or so years. Though there was some overlap, of course."

"It sounds like a horror movie," she told me. *Freaks and Geeks with Creeps*. Or *Nightmare at Predator High*."

"Yeah, it was a nightmare," I agreed. "Though it's been energizing in a weird sort of way, getting involved with this group. I mean, finding out that there were others who'd been through this, that I had this awful thing in common with them. . . ."

She wanted more information about how such activities could go on for so long without any public disclosure or protests by school parents . . . but I really didn't feel like discussing it further. In fact I regretted making the call in the first place. (I could have savored this beautiful day for a few minutes more!) And besides, it was already past time for me to get going to Poet's House (funny name, that), where I was going to meet six other members of my group for the first time, to be part of a public panel discussion. "I'll write you an email," I told her and disconnected.

It was four o'clock now, and the sun was going down. There was a chill in the air. I tried to recapture the tranquil state of mind I'd been in before, but it was no use. Pressing matters were back, and the group was waiting. I couldn't delay any longer.

Part One

CHAPTER 1

IF AMERICA IS INDEED "A SHINING CITY ON A HILL" (as Ronald Reagan described it), then Horace Mann School—with its ivy-covered stone and brick buildings impressively nestled at the top of 246th Street in the Bronx, NY, looking down on the world—could well be called America's prep school. That's certainly how I remember feeling when I was in seventh grade (or First Form, as it was called there) and attending my first chapel service in the cavernous school auditorium with 120 or so other twelve-year-old boys. (At that time the school was still single sex; it became co-educational twelve years later, in 1977.)

"I look out at you today, and I don't see a group of young boys," the chaplain intoned. "I see the doctors and lawyers and statesmen of tomorrow. I see the congressmen and senators and leaders of tomorrow. Who knows—maybe even a future president of the United States is with us today." (We looked around at each other, smiles of embarrassment or smugness on our faces, depending on how high an opinion of ourselves each of us had.) "Yes, you are America's future—or you can be if you work hard and take advantage of the opportunity you have been given. Don't let your parents down, don't let yourself down—or you will regret it for the rest of your lives." The chaplain looked around piercingly at all of us, as if staring into our pre-teen souls; then he told us to take out the sheet of paper we had been handed, and he led us in singing a Christian hymn.

Many things about this experience struck me as strange, perhaps foremost being that the chaplain was a small Asian man named Mr Lin. (At that time, we would still have used the word "Oriental" to describe him.) I had never seen an Asian teacher before. In fact, I don't remember seeing many Asian people in my daily life who weren't workers in Chinese restaurants or Chinese laundries. This is a cliché, I know, but at the time it was also a fact for a middle class kid growing up on the upper West Side of New York City. So it intrigued me to see this Asian man in a position of authority, especially as a voice of Christianity. I had never known any Asian Christians before, had never even thought about the possibility. Asians at that time were very much "the other" in American society. They rarely appeared on TV. When they did, it was usually as anonymous "Chinamen" with bit parts in Westerns, helping to build the railroad or (again) doing the laundry.

I had heard that Mr Lin was also an English teacher, but for the next two years I knew him only as the chaplain who presided over the chapel assembly we were forced to attend once a week. The fact that at least 80% of the students were Jewish just added to the oddness of these occasions. I was bored to tears by most Jewish religiosity, but at least that was my religion. To sit there week in and week out and listen to Mr Lin drone on in his snappish and self-satisfied way about the glories of God was not to my taste at all. But then singing these Christian hymns—"A Mighty Fortress is our God" and so forth—even to my twelve- or thirteen-year-old self, this was a boredom beyond endurance, and it led to an unexpected encounter with the high-minded chaplain himself.

I was in eighth grade at the time, and I was angry at myself for botching a test—probably in math or history, though that's just a guess. This caused me to be oblivious of Mr Lin's sermon on that particular day, and then—finally released from Jesus prison—I crumpled the hymnal sheet into a ball and sent it sailing (by a one-handed set shot) toward the narrow opening of a dark four foot high garbage container. The balled-up hymn sheet went right into the opening on a perfect arc. Just as I was raising my hands in the air and saying the word "Yes!" something surprising happened, something very much like those lightning bolts from on high that the Lord was fond of hurling at this or that sinner.

Now there was one thing about Mr Lin that I genuinely respected—he was an ardent pacifist. My mom was a pacifist too, so much so that she wouldn't let me or my three younger brothers play with toy guns or other simulated weapons. (Her efforts were fairly useless, of course, as everyone knows that a boy can make a weapon out of a stick, a stone, a zucchini—pretty much anything. But I guess it was the thought that counted.) On that particular day, though, the Mr Lin I experienced was anything but pacifistic.

He grabbed me hard by the left earlobe, and, before I knew what was happening, the diminutive Mr Lin began dragging me around the campus, through the hallways of the school buildings.

"Please—stop—don't—I'm sorry—that really hurts" (or words to that effect), I pleaded.

Every time we rounded a corner, I got a view of Mr Lin's face looking grimly ahead, never glancing at me, never heeding my pleas for mercy. Meanwhile, older boys pointed at me and laughed, enjoying my misery. A few times we encountered a logjam of students blocking our way. Mr Lin barked out commands for the path to be cleared as he dragged me with unswerving relentlessness through one building, down a number of steps, across a stretch of pavement and into another stone building. Small as he was, I often had to run to keep up, and it hurt like hell when I'd fall behind and he'd tug really hard on my ear. (And through it all I just remember those faces of upper classmen, grotesquely distorted faces, as amused by my plight as if I'd been all four Marx Brothers rolled into one.)

Our hero's journey landed us in Tillinghast Hall—the main hub of the school—as Mr Lin pulled me up a number of exterior steps, inside a swinging door, up a dark staircase, then into the office of the Headmaster, Doctor Gratwick. I remember seeing the Headmaster's secretary look up with surprise as I went whizzing past. She started to say something to Mr Lin (I had become just a prop, a thing with no selfhood at all), but he marched past, grimly determined, a man on a mission. This ended with Mr Lin throwing me down by my earlobe into a seat in front of the headmaster's very large desk.

"This boy has to be punished," Mr Lin snorted, eyes blazing.

"What has he done?" Dr Gratwick asked, looking at me with hooded eyes.

"He desecrated school property," Mr Lin answered, pursing his lips.

"Is that true?" Dr Gratwick asked me.

"It was a song sheet," I blurted out. "I just . . . threw it away."

"You crumpled it up like it was garbage," Mr Lin hissed.

I wish I could say that I was trying very hard not to laugh—given how ludicrous all this seems now—but the truth is, I was trying hard not to cry. I was a conscientious student, had never been in trouble before, and had—in fact—been the president of my First Form class. Add to this that my ear was still stinging like crazy and this peace-loving chaplain stood over me with eyes blazing and nostrils flaring, and I guess it's not surprising that the impulse to cry was proving so hard to quell. But it was this headmaster that really had me quavering. He was so old, so very old and gray, with his gray suit and gray hair and grayish-tinged skin and the gray way he was looking at me with those hooded eyes. Even his name sounded gray—"Gratwick." I was terrified.

"I believe this is your first offense?" the headmaster asked.

I nodded.

Dr Gratwick reached into his top left desk drawer, took out a tan manila folder, opened it and made a notation on a piece of paper. Then he looked to his right at Mr Lin and nodded slightly.

"Thank you for bringing this to my attention, Mr Lin," he intoned. "I'm sure it will never happen again. Isn't that right, Mr Fife?"

I nodded again, tears starting to stream down the left side of my face, despite my best efforts to suppress them.

"Can I hear you apologize to Mr Lin?" Dr Gratwick said, looking at me.

I took a quick gulp of air, glanced at Mr Lin (who was glaring at me) and said, "Sorry, Mr Lin—" before my voice broke, and I let out a sob— but was able to stop before breaking down any further.

"Thank you, Dr Gratwick," Mr Lin said, then left the room.

Dr Gratwick picked up the tan manila folder, looking it over.

"This is a serious offense, Mr Fife, a very serious offense. We take desecration of school property seriously here," Dr Gratwick droned. "But since this is your first time in my office, I will not put a black mark on your college record."

"Thank you, sir," I said.

"And I won't tell your parents about this incident either," he intoned. "It will just be our little secret. Unless of course I see you in here again."

"Thank you, sir. No, that won't happen, I promise, sir," I stammered, like some pathetic character from a Dickens novel. ("Please, sir, can I have another?")

I felt relief spreading over me like a soothing ointment, a sense of being reprieved. It was great news that colleges would never have to learn that I was a wonton paper-crumpler, a desecrator of song sheets. But it was much better news that my parents wouldn't be told. I dreaded my dad asking me, "What is this I hear about your getting in trouble?" But that was nothing compared to my mom's "We are so disappointed in you!" and "How could you do this?" She had a way of asking a question like that which was akin to the sound of a dump truck backing up before it buried you in a shitload of guilt.

Of course it was my mom's idea that I attend Horace Mann in the first place. I was perfectly happy at the grade school which I had attended from First to Sixth grade, a small co-ed private school on the privileged upper West Side which had an adjoining middle and upper school. I was a good student, friends with everyone in my class, a star athlete and a good actor, as well as a little flirt with all the girls. I had been elected president of the class every year there had been an election. In fact, I'd never lost an election for anything in my young life, not in school, in summer camp, in cub scouts or in Hebrew school (Best Dreydel Spinner!). Given that my mom was a rising political star—democratic state committeewoman and co-chair of the Liberal Democratic Club—there seemed no doubt about what I was intended to be.

I suppose that brings us back to Mr Lin's "future leaders of America" speech and why my mom had me apply in the first place to this shining high school on the hill. And I didn't disappoint. I was elected President of the First Form, my sense of political entitlement remaining intact. But this was a highly competitive, all-male environment—nothing warm and fuzzy here, no empathetic girls to help me through the hard times, and one year of being a standing target for boys as smart or smarter than me was quite enough, thank you. The next year I ran for school assembly from my homeroom—and won easily. But that's when things started to change in a big way.

First, there was the ear-tugging incident with Mr Lin, which cracked the bubble of security that I'd been living within during my first eighteen months at the school. After the shock of my public humiliation had worn off, I started feeling the injustice of what I'd been put through. And suddenly I realized that nobody here was on my side. I wasn't special or cared about or respected; in fact, I was treated like I was worthless, and I didn't seem to have any rights.

My fragile bubble of entitlement was shattered completely just a month later when I ran for re-election to the school assembly and lost. Yes, lost my first election, and in a homeroom, no less. How was my streak snapped? Because I took my voters—I mean, my friends—for granted and made it seem like my victory was a foregone conclusion. At the time I felt betrayed, and I wept like a pre-schooler. (The tears that I'd managed to hold back in the headmaster's office now flowed all too freely.) But all these years later I understand that my classmates were absolutely right. And whatever message they might have been sending about my being an arrogant prick, they also set me free from my pre-determined destiny, allowing me to explore alternate pathways that I might never have had the courage to pursue on my own. For this I am profoundly thankful—even if it did end up delivering me right into the waiting arms of Horace Mann's two writing gurus and a darker side of human nature than (even with my rapidly-expanding sense of imagination) I could ever have imagined.

CHAPTER 2

IN THE LATE 1960S THE WORLD WENT A LITTLE CRAZY, and so did a lot of young people, myself included. Bobby Kennedy and Martin Luther King were assassinated. There was rioting at the Democratic convention in Chicago as the unjust war in Vietnam raged on, and all of this was broadcast right into our comfortable, middle-class living rooms. Like so many other teens, I started writing poetry about how screwed-up the world was. I got involved in raising money for the starving people of Biafra, and I went to a social work camp in Louisville, Kentucky, where I hooked up with an anti-war group who smuggled me and three of my friends into Fort Knox, where we handed out anti-military literature and were arrested and thrown into the brig. The next year I took part in the March on the Justice Department in Washington, DC, where I held a candle and wore the name of a dead soldier around my neck and was tear-gassed while racing across Independence Plaza, out-running the helmeted National Guard troops and then helping to "liberate" a movie theatre that was showing *Monterey Pop. . . .*

I could also throw in how I smoked a joint with Yippie leader Abbie Hoffman and went backstage at an anti-war concert to meet Jimi Hendrix and was also fortunate enough to meet Bobby Kennedy and Eugene McCarthy and took part in a number of other events that went along with those tumultuous times—but, looking back on it now, I'd have to say that the major event in my life back then, the major turning point, was finally getting my own bedroom at home, after years of sharing with one or another of my brothers. It was a great day when at fifteen I got that deeply-desired room of my own—but also a weird one, in ways that I didn't understand at the time and still can't completely make sense of.

The thing I didn't realize then—and in fact only became aware of years later, in my early forties—was that this bedroom behind the family kitchen came with a history and a whole lot of baggage. The fact was—and this is one of those times when there are no words, or at least not the right ones—I had been molested in this room's adjoining bathroom when I was seven- and eight-years-old by a 300 pound West Indian house-keeper named Nina who my parents employed for several months as a housekeeper. When my parents went out to dinner parties on Saturday evenings—as they often did—Nina would turn on the faucets in this bathroom and set a bath. Then she would start addressing my brother Richie (then four or five) and me by her pet names—I was "Skinny on the beach," Richie was "Fat as a water rat." (He wasn't fat, just a normal well fed kid who would thin out when he grew to over six feet.)

She'd start singing out—after we'd been fed, and the dinner dishes had been cleared away—"Come here, Skinny on the beach, it's time for your bath! And time for you to go away, Mr Fat as a water rat! Nobody needs you, nobody wants to see you, fat as you are!" My brother would blush a deep red and start running around in crazy circles, until Nina chased him off to the bedroom that he and I shared.

I tried to resist her, saying I didn't want a bath, and if I did, then I would take it by myself in my own bathroom. I think I may have tried running away to the farthest reaches of the apartment—that isn't very clear to me anymore. What is clear is that I took at least a few baths with her, as I have very strong sense memories of those times—her enormous breasts, each of which seemed as big as I was. Her enormous brown body, the sheer volume of it, the rolls of brown fat. The huge thatch of black pubic hair. Her great big hands taking my small right hand and guiding it toward her nether regions. The grunts and gasps she emitted when I touched her there. How small and inconsequential I felt, sitting in the lukewarm water, goosebumps rising on my pale skin. (She would only fill up the bath a few inches—I'm not sure why, maybe to leave her vagina above water.) I remember her making fun of how small my seven-year-old penis was, and how she wished it was bigger so I could give her pleasure. (Of course I had no idea what she meant—there were only six stations on TV and none showed sexual images of any kind.) I remember being terrified by the disproportion between us, her so giant-sized, me so skinny and frail. And I remember being weirded out when she put my hand inside her—confused, afraid, disgusted, sort of turned on (in a way that I couldn't process) and very ashamed. (It was so warm and wet in there! And so spacious! My little hand flopped around like a fish in a bucket until she pressed it to her particular spot.)

I didn't tell my mother back then—I guess I was just too overwhelmed and confused by how much excitement and shame I felt. Or too afraid of Nina—or maybe of making my mom angry. I don't really recall much other than the physical sensations and images from our interactions, her guiding my small hand into her large orifice and then insisting that I stimulate her. Then suddenly Nina was gone and the bathtub sessions were over, and I didn't think about it again until I was forty-three, when these images and sensations started coming back to me in flashes, mostly during and right after sexual intercourse.

Eventually the images started coalescing into actual scenes, and then the reality of what had happened became crystal clear, the memory emerged like a lost part of myself (which indeed it was), palpable and intact. That was when I did go to my mom and told her what had happened so long ago.

"No, that's impossible," she said. "I fired Nina for being an incompetent housekeeper, but there was never anything like that." Her denial became even stauncher when she checked with my brother Richie, and he had no recollection of any of this. "You must be mistaken," she repeated.

"Yeah, mom, like I'm going to make up something like that," I said.

I mean, no way I could conjure up that giant body, those breasts, the sensation of my small hand sliding into her private parts. If I was going to fantasize about a housekeeper, then there were plenty of others who I would much rather have imagined myself interacting with. No, there are just some things that you have to take on faith, like a thirty-five-year-old memory that no one can do anything about except simply accept the damage already done. But, sadly for both our sakes, my mom couldn't do that.

* * *

So yes, at fifteen-years-old I moved into this room fraught with a terrible personal history that I did not and could not remember. The question that comes to mind—the question that still lingers for me after all these years—is what effect did this history that I was not aware of have on my behavior and development?

The fact is, I was and had been a pretty regular kid in most respects. I liked sports, pined for girls, had plenty of friends. My need to win every election—had that come from feeling so much self-loathing that I needed everyone not just to like me but also to vote for me? Or was that the result of being the oldest of four boys and needing to be reassured that I was still the favorite? Or was it simply because I'd been raised by two socially ambitious parents, one of whom was in fact a politician?

Certainly, compared to my brothers, I seemed to have lots more highs and lows. I was not nearly as grounded and consistent. I had more trouble with impulse control than my brothers seemed to, rendering me more likely to commit rash acts and make split-second decisions. I lashed out physically sometimes, got into a few fist-fights with rivals and even with friends, though I felt terrible afterward because my mom was such a pea-cenik and hated violence. (I might as well have been raised by Quakers, not Jews.) But was this all that unusual for a growing boy, especially one who attended a testosterone-driven all-boys school? Maybe it was differ-ent from my brothers' behavior, but it also did not seem all that abnormal. This was New York City after all, not a wheat field in Kansas. I spent two hours each day on the subway. Things happened.

But there were certain experiences—sexually-tinged experiences—that I'd had, which did seem both different in kind from anything my broth-ers had gone through and fairly strange in themselves. The summer when I was ten, for instance, and my family was living in a rented home on a shady lane in Westport, Connecticut, I had a thin, dark-haired girlfriend, a year younger than me, who lived a few lanes over. Nothing all that unusual there, except that she was obsessed with undressing me, and I kept storm-ing away, then coming back. I recall very vividly spending summer after-noons with her, swinging slowly back and forth in one of those two-person swings, and in the middle of our talking I'd look down at my shorts and find my belt unbuckled and my front snap undone. I would get red-faced and flustered, stand up, fix my clothing, tell her not to do that again. And she would. And the scene would repeat itself. I remember once getting so angry that I scrambled up into her tree-house and pelted her with crab apples until she started crying (when of course I felt terrible—"just don't do that anymore!" I yelled, tearing up). Then again, I recall swimming with her in the Rolling Hills country club pool, where she would grab the back of my bathing suit and threaten to pull it down. "Don't," I pleaded, genuinely terrified of being humiliated. But she enjoyed it too much, this humiliation game, and I eventually had to stop being her friend.

The next year, when I was eleven-years-old and in fifth grade in the small private school that I went to before Horace Mann, a cute red-haired girl that I often flirted with asked me to come over to her house after school. I said, "Sure," and I guess told my parents that I was going to visit a friend. She was a latchkey kid, and her family lived in a large apartment building on the upper West Side. I remember the very unusual feeling of entering the empty apartment with her. I don't think I'd ever been in an empty apartment before, just me and someone my age. She took me by the hand and led me to a room with a large bed that had been stripped of its sheets and had only a mattress cover. "Take off your clothes," she said, starting to undress. I awkwardly followed her example until we were both in our underwear. "Now get on the bed," she said. I obeyed. We kissed and rolled around on the bed for a while. I don't remember much else about it. She had tiny cupcake breasts, hardly developed. I can't recall if I got an erection. There was a lovely late afternoon breeze. Even then it seemed more like a dream than anything that belonged to my real life.

Were these experiences—and a few others in a similar vein—brought about by my having been molested, my innocence violated, the vocabulary of sex introduced prematurely into my personal lexicon? That is, did my having been used by this housekeeper in such a way cause me to send out signals that these girls had picked up? Or were these just youthful experiences that I would have had anyway?

A similar question remains for me regarding my activities in that room I moved into. I recall having torturously vivid fantasies of a naked waif in my closet who would emerge into the moonlight and come over to the bed and sit down on my erect cock. But I've heard other guys talk about similar fantasies at that age, so maybe it was just normal. On the other hand, it was 1969, the age of flower power and free love, and my new bedroom was the only room in my parents' apartment located behind the kitchen, which was a great thing if you wanted to sneak a girl in there for sex—something I started doing not long after moving in.

Where did I meet these girls, you may ask, given that I went to an all-male school? Rallies. Parties. Poetry readings. Central Park. Washington Square Park. The subway. The elevator. The street. The truth is, it wasn't really that hard to get laid back then if you were sufficiently resourceful, as I appear to have been. All the girls I met were on the pill, there were no incurable STDs to worry about, pot and hash were cheap and plentiful.

So how exactly did it work, you may ask—having sex in this middle-class family apartment with my parents and brothers around?

Well, it went like this: my mom was reassured by the girl that her parents knew where she was and had no problem with it. (A lie that was only made possible by the sincerity of horny girls and the absence of anything like the Internet.) The girl would start out by sleeping in my youngest brother Andy's room, where I used to sleep before moving into my own room. At a certain point, when Andy and everyone else in the house was asleep, the girl would get up and come into my room, where the fun would ensue. It would continue until around five or six in the morning, when the girl would return to Andy's room. Occasionally the girl and I would both fall asleep, and then we'd wake up to the sound of voices in the kitchen. Not good. We'd have to wait until the voices went away, then I'd tiptoe out and make sure the coast was clear. (Hopefully the girl had brought her clothes and overnight bag with her into my room; if not I'd have to sneak into Andy's room and collect them, which could get tricky.) Then I'd walk the girl out the back door, go down in the elevator with her and walk her to the subway. Then I'd go home and make up a story.

Not surprisingly, my parents weren't happy about any of this. Though, truthfully, the only thing my dad would notice was if the phone was off the hook, in which case he'd throw a fit. (Even though he was probably the one who'd left it off.) Otherwise his attitude seemed to be: he had fathered four boys and made a good living selling imitation leather goods, so wasn't that enough? My mom was a very accomplished woman, a graduate of Bryn Mawr and a force in the Liberal Democrat party. The last thing she wanted to be was a police person, checking up on me, but eventually it got to the point where she pleaded with me to ease off. "It's making your brothers uncomfortable," she said. "Okay," I promised, getting red-faced. And I did make an effort to be more discreet after that.

The question again comes up, of course—was I just a lustful teenager or did my prior experiences in this room have something to do with my behavior? I wish I could choose one with some certainty, but how can I? It's a mystery to me too. But I did start having trouble sleeping, and when I slept, my sleep was full of nightmares. I often felt like the walls were closing in. The only thing I could do then to make it better was to write poetry. It was still mostly teenage stuff, full of "breast-white moons" and "flaming sunsets," but I was very serious about it, finding a nascent sense of self that made me feel somewhat less hopeless, a bit less alone.

Chapter 3

IN MY SOPHOMORE YEAR AT HORACE MANN, I had English class with my old pal, the ear-tugger himself, Tek Young Lin. If life was a Hollywood movie, then Mr Lin and I would have met up again, older and wiser, and become fast friends. Or we would have learned to appreciate each other's virtues and different points of view. Or we would at least have shaken hands (metaphorically-speaking) and put our past conflicts behind us. Ah, but life is not a Hollywood movie, and I didn't like his prickly, self-satisfied style, and he didn't like mine either. I remember nothing about the class except him darting around the room, watering his plants, and I didn't save any of the essays I wrote for him. I was writing poetry obsessively, but I never showed him a thing, as I hadn't with my previous year's teacher either—a tall man with a high forehead who put everyone in mind of an undertaker. The creep factor was way too high to have risked revealing my inner thoughts.

Over the summer of 1969, a favorite uncle of mine had died suddenly of a heart attack. He was a nice, uncomplicated man, a dentist who liked to take me fishing with him. I wasn't really the fishing type, but he was a good person who had lost one of his two sons to leukemia. The son of his who died had been an aspiring magician, and I had gone onstage with him when I was around three. (My mom had a photo of it.) It wasn't a huge connection, but I was sad when my uncle died and wrote a poem.

> FOR MY UNCLE WHO DIED
> my night was shaken
> by his stillness;
> a sea was tossed,
> then calm.
> embrace your shock and sorrow;
> cry. please.
> lament your lost relative—
> you should. you must.

honest days of fishing and sport,
and i savored his old salt smile.
no bites
but one
we should have thrown back.
lazy, no-work days of men,
and i never fished
except in that lake
rippled still
with silver hairs of praise.
shapeless cap
and overalls of baggy white.
two children in a child's dream.
these tears are for fish memories
not for sorrow.

I had heard from some friends in the class above me that the English teacher to get for poetry was Robert Cullen. He was a William Blake scholar and a poet himself, as well as being the advisor to the school literary magazine, *The Manuscript*. But when I showed up for my Junior year, I found myself assigned to a different teacher, one who I had heard nothing but terrible things about—and it was hate at first sight. I was attracted to literature for depth, pain, soulfulness, magic and truth; for the indelible word or phrase that opened up worlds within unseen worlds for the imagination. This teacher had a businessman's sense of literature, books were so many bolts of cloth to him—or bolts of imitation leather, like my dad sold. I didn't want anything to do with business or politics, just beauty and truth. As soon as the class was over, I high-tailed it a few doors down the hall to Cullen's classroom. Luckily for me, he was there.

Robert Cullen was a tall-ish man with long strands of brown hair combed back from a high forehead, fuzzy eyebrows and a mad look in his eyes. He always seemed to me like a defrocked priest, pursued by visions of a God he could no longer believe in. His manner was thoughtful, genuine, kind—and somehow haunted, even strange. I had heard he was wealthy, that he had resigned from a cushy corporate job to do what he loved. (In fact, he was the sole heir to the King Kullen supermarket fortune; but I only discovered this many years later.)

I told Mr Cullen my dilemma, and he nodded pensively. Then he asked to see the poems that I'd been writing. I had copies of two or three on me (including *My Uncle Who Died*), and I handed these over.

The next day I was handed a note to go see Mr Cullen. He told me that the transfer was done, and I was officially his student. He also said that he liked my poems and was going to make sure they got printed in *The Manuscript*. Finally, he recommended that I take the opportunity to sign up for classes with another English teacher too—"the most remarkable teacher I've ever encountered, perhaps the most remarkable man as well"—named Robert Berman.

Berman? Oh, I'd been hearing weird things about him since I began going to the school. Rumors, so many rumors. The most often repeated one had two variations: 1) Horace Mann used to have boys swim in the nude in the pool (this part was true), and Berman would lurk on the balcony, taking photos. 2) Berman was wont to sneak into the boy's shower room and snap photos. Both of course had to do with him invading privacy and snapping photos of naked boys. This struck a nerve when I first heard it in seventh grade, tapping into the visceral fear at that age of being humiliated by having one's nakedness made public. (This was long before cell phones and the Internet, so it wasn't even clear how or where these naked photos would be distributed; though that didn't make the anxiety any less intense.) But as the years went on, and I never saw any evidence to substantiate the rumors about Berman, then this boogeyman image faded away. But hearing his name brought up like this by Mr Cullen made me feel queasy, as the memory of that past fear returned in a rush. Nevertheless, I was Cullen's student now, and if he recommended that I take Mr Berman's class, then I would do so.

When I had a free moment, I bounded up the two flights of stairs and entered Mr Berman's classroom. There was indeed a weird vibe here, something different; a seriousness, even a hush. I found that kind of appealing. But Berman himself—wow. Very different. Dark suit, white shirt, dark tie; short, around 5'5", with a shaved head and thick black-framed glasses. He had an affected way of speaking, as if each word had to be pulled out of him. Every movement and gesture seemed to be calculated and controlled, so that he used the least amount of energy necessary to create a desired impression. And there was something oddly otherworldly about him, like a monk in a religious order.

"Mr Cullen has already spoken to me about you, Mr Fife," Mr Berman said, as if my explanation of events had bored him beyond endurance. "The paperwork has already been filed, and you are enrolled in my class on *Hamlet* and *Oedipus*," he said wearily.

Really? It had? Why was I the last to know?

Berman half-smiled (or was he frowning?) cryptically, then he ushered me out and closed the door, as if he couldn't stand a minute more of my wasting his precious time.

Chapter 4

A FTER HAVING STARTED OUT AS MISTER POPULAR—President of my class, back-slapper extraordinaire!—I had shifted around between friendships with different classmates, as I struggled to find a new identity. My best friend for eighth and ninth grades was a boy named Ethan Cole. He was good company, fun to hang around with and very smooth with girls. Ethan was remarkably good-looking—especially for a young Jewish boy. In case you haven't noticed, young Jewish men tend to be physically most awkward just when we're required to stand up in front of the world and declare ourselves to be a man—albeit a very small ugly man with zits on his nose and a high-pitched scratchy voice that makes even loved ones wince. I was a prime example of the breed (once again), especially when I still had thick, multi-layered metal braces on my teeth. The horrible thing was, I kept going around and smiling like I was still the cute kid I had been in grade school, when in fact I now made Quasimodo look like a catch.

So yes, Ethan was very good-looking, amazingly so since his dad had a large nose and his mom was nothing special in the looks department. Ethan was trim but muscular with thick blond hair that cascaded into his eyes. He would clear the hair from his eyes with a flick of his head that I envied. My hair was mousy-brown and wavy and wiry and formed into silly clumps— what we would now call a "Jew-fro," if we were so inclined. Why couldn't I have beautiful blond hair like Ethan's that moved when I flicked it? (All mine did was sit there, stubbornly matted.) Girls flocked to Ethan when we walked down the street, his easy smile and careless manner were like a drug, producing a bleary-eyed look on their eager young faces. I hung back a few steps, hoping to catch the overflow—mostly sad-eyed Jewish girls with hair as clumpy as mine, often with braces in their mouths too, who were too smart (and too accustomed already to disappointment) to fool themselves into believing that Ethan would ever be theirs. I made out with a number of these girls, our braces clacking together or inadvertently inter-locking. ("Ouch! Oh, that hurts." "Don't pull, that just makes it worse!")

And what did Ethan get from me? Let's just say he wasn't the sharpest tool in the drawer (feel free to insert whatever cliché makes you happy there). I helped Ethan with his homework, especially Math and Science, he helped me to get girls and to feel more confident around them—that was the basis for our hanging out. Also, Ethan was an only child, and he wasn't the type who liked to spend time alone, he needed an audience. For my part, I was glad to get away from the crowded family apartment that was so rife with sibling rivalries. And the competition for my mom's affection and attention was not just with my three younger brothers. My dad was less like a father and more like a possessive older sibling, who—whenever he wasn't shouting at some business associate on the phone, which was most of the time—wanted my mom all to himself. I felt caught in the middle, as awkward in this family arrangement as I was in my changing body, which was suddenly sprouting hair and zits and looking more grotesque every day.

My friendship with Ethan somehow survived the summer between eighth and ninth grades, when we were part of an Outward Bound group that traveled around the US, and he consistently—one might say obsessively—stole every girlfriend away from me. Every one that is except Calee, this crazy red-headed girl from Chicago who would make out with me on the side of a steep mountain or as we were almost drowning from having tipped over our canoe on the Snake River—even giving me a hand-job during a torrid rainstorm, when both our tents had collapsed, and we ran off into the forest, where wolves or bears should certainly have eaten us (not that I cared at that moment). At other times, normal times, she was cold as ice and wouldn't even let me sit next to her in the van. No, she was too strange for Ethan—not that this stopped him from trying. He ambushed her one twilight when she was walking through the woods, looking for dry twigs and sticks for that evening's campfire. From what I could piece together, he got her on the ground and had stuck his hand up her sweatshirt and under her bra when she kicked him hard in the nuts. Ethan wasn't heard from for a few days after that, and he wisely never went near her again.

Things with Ethan finally ended in the ninth grade in a rather odd way. Ethan invited me to come with him and his family to Nassau in the Bahamas for winter vacation. The fact that we were only fourteen didn't matter there—we were able to rent motor scooters and drink *pina coladas* to our heart's content. We motored around the island from morning to evening, swilling rum drinks and looking for girls to pick up. Eventually we came upon two beautiful girls our age, sunning themselves on the beach in tiny bikinis. One had blond hair past her shoulders, the other had short dark brown hair in a pixie cut and deeply-tanned skin. "Okay, I'll take the blond, you take the other," Ethan told me. I shrugged my assent, as I usually did. It was no use disagreeing with Ethan, as he never relented. To my great surprise, the girls were happy to see us and agreed right away to get on the back of our scooters. The parents of the girl with the pixie haircut (Susan) had rented a place about a mile and a half away, and they were out for the afternoon. Susan said we could go there.

We zipped over to the pleasant bungalow that Susan's parents had rented, at which point Ethan and the blond adjourned into one bedroom while Susan and I went into another. Susan and I kissed for a few minutes, then she informed me that she was a virgin and had no intention of losing that to me. I was a virgin too then (which I didn't tell her), but I said that was fine, no big deal. We then went back to kissing, but soon began talking too. She was a very bright girl with a great smile and a sweet sense of humor, and she used the word "skill" the way we currently use the word "cool." "That's skill, man, really skill!" she'd say, when I told her about something I liked. It turned out that she read a lot of poetry too, and we both liked Keats and e.e. cummings. "It's so skill that you like poetry too," she said, smiling. "I don't meet many boys who do."

Just then her blond friend came bursting into the room, hair severely tousled, tears in her eyes. "I'm leaving," she told Susan. "See you later."

"Wait. What happened?" Susan asked.

"Don't go," I said. "We can go back to the beach if you want."

The blond girl seemed nervous, she turned around and started heading out, but she ran right into Ethan, who was really miffed.

"What's the idea?" he said. "I go take a piss, when I come back you aren't there!"

"I have to go," the blond girl told him and tried to get past, but Ethan held on. "Let go of me!" she cried.

"No," Ethan said and wrapped his arms around her, trying to give her a kiss.

"Get off me!" the blond girl screamed, wedging her forearm against Ethan's shoulder, pushing him off. Then she dashed out the screen door, slamming it behind her.

"What did you do?" I asked Ethan.

"Nothing!" he said loudly, annoyed. Then turning to Susan: "What's wrong with your friend?"

"Nothing," she said defensively. "She's a great girl. Really fun."

"Fun?" Ethan asked, shaking his head.

"Well, she can be a little religious . . ." Susan admitted.

When Susan left the room, Ethan approached me. He was really angry. "This isn't right," he said. "You're here as my guest, but now I'm the one without a girl."

"Sorry, but that's not my fault," I told him.

Ethan then demanded that we "share" Susan. "It's only fair," he said.

"No way," I told him. "Don't even try it."

But when Susan came back, Ethan sat down next to her on the sofa and started caressing her hair. "Don't," she said. "I don't like that."

"How do you know until you try it?" he cooed.

Soon Susan and I were both shouting at Ethan, while he was shouting back at us.

Eventually Susan and I exchanged addresses, then Ethan and I took off on our scooters, no longer on speaking terms. We were never really friendly again. In fact, I don't recall ever saying another word to him once we got back to school.

I kept in touch with Susan from Nassau for quite a while, writing letters back and forth for the next year and a half or so. I think I had it in mind that she would be the girl I would lose my virginity with. Her family moved around quite a bit, and I believe this is ultimately what defeated that particular plan, as I lost the location of my long-distance pen pal. Then again, maybe she just concluded that I wasn't the one she wanted to be her first. In any case, I do recall quite vividly how, two years later, I slept with a girl named Nora.

She was strikingly beautiful, with jet-black hair and pale white skin. Worthy of an alabaster statue in the Louvre with the title "Artemis, Goddess of the Hunt" or "Hippolyta, Shedding her Girdle," and with just as much warmth. She told me that her dad had abandoned her and her mom when Nora was small, and that her mom had brought her up to take revenge on men. I found this hard to believe. And her mom seemed pleasant enough, too, until she started making comments about "young boys who only want one thing, and they expect to get it, or else."

I told Nora that she couldn't let her mom ruin her life—not when she was just starting out on her own. Nora's response was to break up with me.

"You can't do that," I said, because the next week was the Woodstock Music Festival, which she and I had planned to attend together. Nora informed me that she'd already made other plans—she was going with an ex-friend of mine named Josh, they had already arranged for a ride and had bought matching sleeping bags. "What? How is this possible?" I said, boldly entering the competition for Stupidest Man in New York City. And then I added: "I didn't even know you knew Josh." (Ding ding ding ding ding—and I think we have a winner! Will somebody please bring out the cement shoes for the Jewish lad over there?)

Reigning Prince of Stupidity that I was, I couldn't get Nora out of my mind. I knew she was bad news, I knew that nothing good could happen if we got back together, and yet I couldn't stay away. So, yes, I called Nora again and asked her to come out with me for a weekend on Fire Island. She accepted.

There was supposed to be adult supervision—we would be staying in a small beach cottage owned by friends of my parents, a prominent political couple who would be there as well. They had given me a key, in case I got there before them. Then, at the last minute, the adult couple was unable to go, so Nora and I spent the weekend alone and unsupervised. Two horny teenagers in their own private beach cottage—which may be the definition of Happiness.

We made love, walked on the beach, then made love again. Then we rustled up some food, made love, watched the sunset and made love, then ate something, brushed our teeth, and made love again. There were no cell phones then, of course, and we didn't answer the phone when it rang. For one glorious weekend we were blissfully free of the adult world, in our own island paradise, our own "Blue Lagoon."

Not surprisingly, I suppose, that was the last time I saw Nora. Around a week later she called up to tell me that she was going out with a sophomore in college who could satisfy her better than I did. The smart response would simply have been to be grateful for the twenty or so times we'd made love that weekend and to chalk up the rest to experience; but again, I wasn't winning any awards for brightness back then. I cried bitterly and felt decimated by her rejection. Destroyed. How could she dump me like that? How could she hurt me so badly? We were Adam and Eve, our young bodies perfect in their smooth-skinned innocence, our young minds uncynical and open to all the inspiration of the universe.

In Mr Cullen's class, he gave us an assignment to write a short essay about a recent memory. I wrote about Nora.

SHE

Nora is not yet a memory. She exists in my present mind, thriving within me on the love and warmth I lavish upon her. Though she remains somewhere in a distant port yet unfound in the realm of my travels, I have known her better in the enlightened moments that we have shared than I have known anyone else in this vast world. I shall always think of her as one so close beside me, even when her path leads apart from mine.

The supreme moment of my existence, and thus of my relationship with Nora, has been the weekend I spent with her in a wooden cottage on Fire Island—alone. While on the ferry rolling toward the misty shore, we were seized by a compulsion to smile, for the joy of being amid the salty waves was enormous. I seemed to draw strength from these waves that leapt like dolphins, as if bringing nature back to the body. Standing there upon the paint-chipped deck, soaked with spray in the chilly haze, I felt pangs of remorse well up inside me, for the pangs of love I felt overwhelmed me. I wished these moments to be immortal, and in my soul they are preserved as a perfect poem, as a heart-shaped sound that never ceases.

The cottage stood bold and weatherworn on crystals of windblown sand. The ocean winds blew with the strength of countless men, and our dwelling became a fortress, a landmark of personal freedom. We needed no quarrels to decide the affairs of home, for nature was our judge—the wisest sage man has ever known.

We drifted like two fallen leaves along the ebbing shoreline, far away from the shadows of our homes. Gazing into the sunset's crimson eye, I envisioned among the fleecy clouds a shrine sacred amid night's cold ashes, a shrine where loners and lovers who have perceived an uncommon beauty in the dying of the day are conceived newborn with every setting sun.

Suddenly I squeezed her hand with great force—as if Nora had become nature herself and so would die when the night arrived. She asked me if there was anything wrong, if there were reasons for my sadness. But I could not answer. Once more great throbs of joy overtook my soul, mixed with lonely tears. The mischievous demon of love—who has deceived so many and shall continue doing so until eternity—sprang from the inner reaches of my heart and strangled the words unuttered within my throat. Then, as my lips met hers, I could see—as if a spirit had risen from the waters and opened my eyes—that she too felt this sadness, overcome with intense personal grief. There had been a bond sewn with lasting fibers between our souls, and we were united in a moment of solitude.

Through the blaze of every sunset, we walk in stillness past the flames. Upon the black waters we follow a path as bright as dawn.

Love's demon still plays in passionate fits. No, Nora is not yet a memory.

I didn't have another close friend at school until the start of my junior year, when suddenly I had three. Mitch Bronfman, David Burstein and Justin Strom had been in classes with me for years, though we had rarely spoken. But all three were in Cullen's and Berman's classes, and we soon found that we had a lot in common—a fondness for the written word, a basic curiosity about culture, and really bad relationships with our dads. We also were all pretty much outcasts within our class. I guess today we'd be called "literary nerds," or something like that. But we didn't think of ourselves as "nerds"—more like adventurers of the imagination, trying on ideas and concepts for size . . . which I guess is pretty nerdy, now that I think of it.

A few weeks into our junior year, Mr Berman requested all four of us to stay after class. He then asked if we would be interested in taking a creative writing class with him—just the four of us. We eagerly agreed. This cemented the bond between us—a bond that was soon to be sorely tested.

Chapter 5

MIDWAY THROUGH THE FIRST SEMESTER of my junior year at Horace Mann, the Fall edition of the school's literary magazine, *The Manuscript*, was published, containing three poems of mine.

This may have been a relatively minor event to the world, in a year that included the ascendance of Richard Nixon to president, the undoing of Ted Kennedy at Chappaquiddick, the marriage of John & Yoko, the Manson Family murders, the Woodstock Festival (aaargh!), the resignation of Charles de Gaulle, the Stonewall riots in downtown NYC, Hurricane Camille, the trials of the Chicago Eight, and the My Lai Massacre, the convictions of the assassins of Robert Kennedy and Martin Luther King, and, of course, the Moon Landing and Neil Armstrong's moonwalk (giving ten-year-old Michael Jackson an idea for a badass new dance step!). But, yes, it was a very big event for me, and I burned with anxiety every time I saw a fellow student reading a copy.

Of course, time swallows up most things—except for those six or so people in the world with total recall, poor souls—and I don't remember what any of my schoolmates had to say about my first published poems. Mr Cullen was encouraging, he even told me that his ex-wife loved the one about my dead uncle. Mr Berman said nothing. My mom was very excited, as moms tend to be at such moments, but especially because mine had written her Senior thesis at Bryn Mawr on Romantic Poetry, and she had instilled a love of poetry by reading Wordsworth, Keats, Shelley, and Byron to me when I was growing up. (I never was much for Byron—Keats is the one who has stuck.) My dad said something like, "Congratulations—quite an accomplishment." I did see him reading a copy, which made me shake with nervousness, but I never heard any response.

Oddly enough, *The Horace Mann Record* (the school's newspaper, very much modeled on the *New York Times*) had this issue of the literary magazine reviewed not once but twice. The first review was pretty negative for the issue as a whole, calling it "slim pickings," but it praised me for "colorful and imaginative metaphors and an unusual sensitivity and verbal power." The second review was written by Johannes Somary, the head of the Music Department. He liked the issue better than the first reviewer and found three of the published poems to be "beautiful." Two of them were mine, *For My Uncle Who Died* and *Where*, which he wrote, "snigs [sic], stings and rings with fervor and warmth" as it chronicles "the unpredictable workings of the mind." This is the poem:

> *WHERE*
> *Frozen and fated*
> *The snowdrift flower*
> *Melts within winter's*
> *Clouded breath; unshrouded*
> *From wind madness,*
> *Brotherless and alone.*
> *Slick with sweat, the*
> *Summer petals*
> *Nod and swoon, dust-stained*
> *Among the honey country,*
> *Puckered and curled*
> *Within city swelter.*
> *Shadowed and still*
> *Amid raking leaves, the*
> *Autumn blossom*
> *Sways wary in its wonder,*
> *Clinging to the earth*
> *In a fiery embrace of*
> *Memory and longing.*
> *Instant in innocence, the*
> *Spring seedling*
> *Arises with a world*
> *Thin and starving*
> *For the petal rainbow,*
> *Nurturing nature at her zenith.*
> *My mind is this flower:*
> *An island within me*
> *Alive and weathered*
> *By changing seasons.*

Mr Somary's review in the *Record* begins: "Every man must learn to live creatively with the chaos that exists within him." These words will ring with a strange and cruel irony for anyone familiar with Amos Kamil's article in the June 10, 2012 issue of the *New York Times* entitled *Prep School Predators*. In the piece, Mr Somary is portrayed as "the son of a

famous Austrian-Swiss banker with wild hair and a faraway gaze, almost
a caricature of a brilliant maestro. He enjoyed a prominent international
reputation, having guest-conducted numerous orchestras, including the
Royal Philharmonic of London and the Vienna Philharmonic." The article
chronicles a few serious and horrifying allegations of sexual abuse against
Somary, especially one in 1993 with a student named Ben Balter which resulted in Mr Balter's eventual suicide. But since the article's publication, I
have heard the pain and suffering in the voices of those whom Mr Somary
fondled, kissed, went down on, and sodomized, and I have no doubt that
the events I've listened to them describe actually took place.

For myself—devoid of the talent to play a musical instrument or voice
a pleasing note—I had little to do with Somary, and he had almost no interest in me. I took a required Music class with him and was placed with
the hopeless cases—the equivalent of those kids in Physical Education
who couldn't run the length of the field without tripping over their own
feet. And I was fine with that, even relieved. Public speaking is a breeze
for me, but public singing—oh no. Some of my worst memories are from
my time as an actor, when I was somehow cast in a musical and had to
belt out a song. Ah yes, there's nothing quite like watching a collective
wince pass over an audience like a dark cloud, while thinking to yourself: "Yes, I did that."

But the fact is that Mr Somary escaped unchastised, he taught a long
time at Horace Mann and retired with much fanfare in 2002—even though
Ben Balter's mother, Kathryn Howard, was a Math teacher on the faculty
at Horace Mann. She took her case to the Board of Trustees in 1993, after her son's first suicide attempt, which followed his sending a letter to
the then-Headmaster, detailing Somary's crimes. But the Board sided with
Somary, and nothing changed—Somary went on teaching and abusing
kids, Ben Balter graduated, but he had lost his direction in life and, fifteen
years later, succeeded in ending it.

I am still haunted by that opening sentence of Somary's review: "Every
man must learn to live creatively with the chaos that exists within him."
Is that how Somary "lived creatively" with his "chaos"—by using young
prodigies as his sex toys? By taking the best and the brightest in Horace
Mann's music program and unleashing his darkness on them, to the point
that they could no longer see any light?

There are many things I don't understand about human nature, and this
is certainly one. Especially since Johannes Somary had a beautiful wife
and three lovely, healthy children (who later attended Horace Mann), and
he must have known the legacy of sorrow that he was leaving behind. As

an artist—which he was—and simply as a human being, how can you do that?

* * *

Back in that shining school on the hill, my status was certainly altered for the better by the two reviews, especially the glowing one from Mr Somary. Mr Cullen was very supportive of my work, and he was not shy in saying so. In fact, he somehow arranged for me to go around to various classes, reading my poems aloud to other schoolmates, followed by a discussion. In a competitive environment like Horace Mann's, such an exhibition is fraught with peril. Every boy there was smart and highly motivated to succeed. To have my "achievement" (their word, not mine) thrown in their faces generated a good deal of what would now be called "*schadenfreude*" but then was simply ill-will.

My favorite experience of this kind was a trip back to the classroom that I had transferred out of just two months before, but this time returning in triumph to read my poem about my uncle. The teacher who had openly despised me was now cool and calm, saying nice things about my poem and my "talent." But I could sense him gritting his teeth, and I'm sure he was counting the minutes before I'd be gone. (I've been told by someone who would know that this teacher drank himself to death some years later, and this genuinely saddens me. Teaching is hard, and teaching someone as full of himself as I must have been is especially so.)

One person who seemed oblivious to my change in status was Mr Berman—but then, nothing much appeared to impress him. For those students who liked him, this was one of the main sources of his appeal—he was inured to the fashionable and trendy. He loved Milton, Shakespeare, Dante, Melville, Robert Frost, Dostoievski, Sigmund Freud, Leonardo Da Vinci, Michelangelo and a slew of other Renaissance artists, Mozart, Bach, Beethoven, Schubert, Mahler, Bruckner, Wagner—the classics. He hated TV and all forms of pop culture (or so he claimed). He once memorably remarked: "If the Second Coming were broadcast on television, I still wouldn't watch." The only thing that impressed him was "genius"—as he defined it. And that was something (he made clear) that we students were innately incapable of comprehending.

"You will not write anything worth reading for at least the next twenty years" was the theme of his first lesson to Mitch, David, Justin and me in our creative writing class with him.

"Why even take this class then?" Mitch asked.

"So you can write something worth reading in twenty years," he responded.

"You don't really mean "twenty years" do you?" Justin asked.

"Of course I do," Berman answered. "I wouldn't have said it otherwise."

"Isn't it more like a metaphor for the amount of work it takes to be a good writer?" David followed up.

"If I wanted to use a metaphor, I would have used a metaphor," Berman stated. "What I'm saying is that you shouldn't expect to write anything worth reading before you are forty years old."

"That just sounds silly," I put in, pointing out that Rimbaud wrote *A Season in Hell* when he was a teenager, and F. Scott Fitzgerald wrote all his best work *before* he turned forty. And what about Keats? (He died at twenty-five.)

"Those writers are not your concern. They were geniuses. They are in a category all their own. Much better for you to put in the work now in the hope that you'll write something interesting in the distant future," Mr Berman insisted.

But the first few assignments we wrote for him were not well-received.

"Your work is boring," Berman told us, looking disgusted. "To write an interesting story, you have to start with an interesting subject. *Moby Dick*, on the most basic level, is about the hunt for the greatest of Great White Whales. God looked down on it from heaven, and He approved. No great novel was ever written about the life of the tsetse fly. I want you to think big, not small. I want you to try to build cathedrals, even if they fall down. Or no—*because* they will fall down. But the glory will be in your trying to have done something worth doing, rather than settling as everyone else does for what comes easily. Now go out and start planning how to build your cathedral."

Mr Berman's exhortations led to some lengthy discussions and quite a bit of grumbling among the four of us.

"Do you think he really believes all that stuff, or is he just saying it for effect?" Mitch asked.

"I'm sure he absolutely believes it," David asserted. "Mr Berman is not someone who kids around."

"Yeah, not a big sense of humor there," Justin said.

"Oh, I don't know, I think he enjoys watching us squirm," Mitch said. "I can see a smile playing around the corners of his lips sometimes. He has to work pretty hard to suppress it."

"'A smile playing around the corner of his lips.' I like that," Justin said.

"I'm going to use that in my next story for Berman."

"Go right ahead, steal anything you want, I don't mind," Mitch told him, flashing a grin, obviously pleased by the compliment.

"I know what you mean," I put in, agreeing with Mitch's statement from before. "I can see the hint of a smile there too sometimes. But he's so confident, so sure that he's always right. How can anyone be that sure of himself all the time?"

"Because he's read every book on the planet, and he knows what he knows, and he's completely serious about it," David said. "There's no hint of humor at all."

"'He knows what he knows'" Mitch said mockingly, looking at David. "What does that even mean? It sounds like a tautology."

"You mean a solispsism, not a tautology," Justin corrected.

"No, he means a sophistry," David insisted, and the conversation would devolve from there.

The four of us formed a real unit now, a solid group: The Four Musketeers. "Budding intellectuals"—that is probably a fair description. All of us were Jewish, none of us religiously observant, all definitely tending toward the atheistic or at the very least agnostic. All of us were heterosexual, as far as we knew, though it would be fair to say that there was a subtle homoerotic underpinning to our relations. We talked mostly about literature, philosophy, Renaissance painting and classical music. But none of us painted or excelled at an instrument (though Mitch had a real talent for drawing), so writing and speculating about the purpose of life were the main activities that drew us together. None of them liked sports, so now I didn't either, having left the swim team and my friends on the basketball team in my wake. I didn't watch sports on TV anymore, in fact I didn't watch television at all, after having been a big fan of comedies like *The Honeymooners* and *I Love Lucy* and the variety shows of Ed Sullivan and Jackie Gleason.

(This casting-off of sports and TV was a big blow to my dad and my brothers, as this had always been a primary link between us. My dad had taken us to live sports events all the time—Rangers, Knicks, Yankees, Mets, and (especially) New York Giants games. He had been an athlete in college, on the football and basketball teams, and he gloried in the atmosphere of competitive sports. But now I had no interest in coming along, and the divide between me and my family grew ever greater.)

Within our Gang of Four, there was a definite division of best friends: David and Justin as one subset, Mitch and me as the other. I really didn't know Justin well at all, never went to his home, never met his parents. He was a good-looking guy with straight jet-black hair and tortoise-shell glasses, a good sense of humor, a good but not great writer, who happened to be David's best friend and never caused any real conflict. David was a different story—tall and thin with curly light brown hair and tortoise-shell glasses, he was brilliant and very sensitive, deeply emotional. He was also a talented actor, which I envied, since I loved to act but had become too self-conscious to go out for roles anymore. (I had actually spent some time in my sophomore year running the light-board for *The Little Prince*, just so I could be near the stage and be a part of the production.)

Mitch Bronfman was, to my mind, the coolest and most interesting person in my grade. He had long dark-brown hair parted in the middle, olive skin, perfect features and wore gold wire-rim glasses. He bore an uncanny resemblance to John Lennon as he appeared on the cover of the *Let It Be* album, which had come out the year before. He was smart and funny and much more at ease in his body than me. After the breakup with Nora, I had one night stands with a number of girls my age, then I stopped seeking out girls altogether and brooded a lot about the fickleness of the opposite sex. Mitch never brooded. Even though he was almost a full year younger than me, he was far more sophisticated about sex and didn't really seem to worry about how things were going to turn out. Other kids in our grade thought he was arrogant—or that's what they said. But really they just envied his style, as I did as well. The fact that I was now his best friend (and he was mine) made me happier than anything else in my previous four years at the school.

Sometime during that fall semester, the four of us went along with a few other kids from our school to a Model United Nations Conference held in a midtown hotel on the East Side (near the actual UN). As I recall, we were assigned to represent the great country of Bulgaria. As such, we made a Marx Brothers-inspired mockery of the proceedings, throwing chicken drumsticks at the Soviet Union in protest against their iron-fisted repression. This got us kicked out of the conference hall, but it made a name for us with the other kids at the event. That night many of the participants stayed over in the hotel, with David, Justin, Mitch and me all sharing a room. Several kids wandered over to find out who these wild kids were who had made such a ruckus. Eventually the crowd thinned out, and we were just about to go to sleep when a lone girl came to our door and walked in. Her name was Lisa, she was lovely with shoulder-length dark hair and bangs and pale skin that turned completely red when she blushed. She drifted in and started talking to us in kind of a serious way about world peace and how much she hated violence. We turned out the light, but she stayed and kept talking in a very heartfelt way. Mitch went over and started making out with her. I thought they had sex, and I could have sworn I heard them climax; but Mitch swears to this day that they didn't, so I guess it was just my over-active imagination at work again.

Lisa gave Mitch her number before she left, but Mitch told me that he didn't really have any interest in following up. I asked if he would mind if I did. He said he didn't and gave me her number. I called, and soon Lisa and I began going out—that is, sleeping together. Her family lived in Rye, New York, outside the city, and I would take a train from Grand Central, and she would meet me in her family's car at the station, as if we were a young married couple. She lived in a blended family with loads of siblings and step-siblings, and they could only spare a fold-out sofa for me. But that was fine, since I didn't really spend any time on it. As soon as the lights were out and the house had fallen quiet, I would sneak down to the family rec-room, where Lisa would be waiting in her white nightgown. The room was dark except for the moonlight flooding in, creating crazy silver shadows over most of the toys and the games that the kids were now too old for and no longer played with.

Where Nora was long and lanky, Lisa was more of an earth-goddess, with ample breasts and thickish knees. For some reason I really loved her knees and remember them vividly, especially the way she would curl up and press them against her body and her lovely breasts after we'd made love.

Where sex with Nora had been hostile and quick, sex with Lisa was slow and affectionate. She was a sweet, generous person with a soft voice and an easy laugh. I admired her personal politics, as she took stands against state-sponsored violence and did what she could to promote the cause of world peace. We had many conversations about how we were going to change the world, and how glorious our futures would be, and all the wonderful things we wanted to do with our lives. But most of all we made love in that playroom, alive with silver-tinged shadows that roamed the walls restlessly while we grappled, then came to rest on our naked bodies as we slept peacefully in each others' arms.

Chapter 6

DESPITE ALL THE INTELLECTUAL HEAVYWEIGHTS whom I'd been studying in that first semester—Shakespeare, Sophocles, Freud, Milton,
Blake, Ernest Jones, to name a few—my favorite author was still
J.D.Salinger, and my favorite piece of writing was a tie between his
novel *Franny and Zooey* and his short story *A Perfect Day for Bananafish*.
My favorite poets were William Carlos Williams and Dylan Thomas. I
mention this only to make it clear that I went to literature primarily for
my heart, not my head. I went for emotional sustenance, to be part of a
community that addressed issues of love, loss, passion, quirkiness, sorrow, disappointment, loneliness, uncertainty—that is, issues of life and
death that weren't usually talked about. And I loved to see this done with
style and imagination by authors who knew how to weave a magic spell
and take me someplace I hadn't been, show me something I hadn't expected and, most of all, make me *feel* something about life that moved me
to laugh or cry (or both), but did not allow me to remain neutral. I know
that such a description could also be employed by fans of Harlequin
Romances and other sentimental fictions. But this was the truth for me,
it was "where I came from" as a would-be author, and it was something
that I would soon lose sight of, to my serious peril.

In a similar way, it's easy from the distance of so many years to talk
about the many youthful love-making experiences I had in a cavalier way,
as if I was some kind of teenage playboy—which could not be further
from the truth. Just as I went to literature for the emotion, I went to young
women for emotional contact, for passion and nurturing, for a sense of
fellowship and warmth and understanding. My parents certainly loved and
cared about me and provided very well for me, but they were measured in
their affections, reserved, and this was not what I needed. I was a lonely
teenager awkwardly looking for love and acceptance. The fact that I had
been molested at such a young age undoubtedly caused me to sexualize
these needs in ways that I probably wouldn't have otherwise. And it also
made me vulnerable to adults with a manipulative bent, something that I
had no awareness of at the time, as I felt very much in charge of my life.

I had experienced this very directly on the streets of New York City
from around the age of fourteen, in a way that none of my younger brothers

apparently ever did. What I'm referring to is being hit on by men, something that I found very confusing. I was a skinny kid with long curly brown hair and some definite authority issues, and I guess this sent out a signal (long before cell phones or the Internet), because sometimes it seemed like every gay man in the city was on this wavelength. I remember one time when I was late fourteen or just barely fifteen and walking on the long block fronting the Museum of Natural History, across the street from Central Park. An older man—by which I mean probably forty—with an expensive camera around his neck approached me and asked if I would be interested in making some extra money. "How?" I asked. Well, he was a professional photographer, and he needed a model for a shoot for a major magazine, and the pay was $100 an hour.

Of course my naïve young mind was immediately filled with images of me in a Brooks Brothers button-down shirt stuffing hundred dollar bills into my slacks pocket—so much so that when the man said he lived right around the corner and would I like to see his portfolio? I said, "Sure, lead the way." The next thing I knew I was walking down three steps into a side street basement apartment, then following this guy I didn't know through a beaded curtain into a small study. There he actually did take out a portfolio (Thank God!) and opened to a black-and-white photo of a dark-haired boy of around fourteen wearing only jockey shorts. "Well, at least he's not naked," I thought, still trying to hang on to a hundred dollar bill or two, but then the man turned the page and—oh no! There was the same boy, naked with his finger up his butt and his business hanging out. And that was by no means the worst of the photos. I stopped the man from turning any more pages. "I can't do that," I said. "I mean, what if my parents saw it?"

The man repeated his offer of money, but even he knew at this point that it was a non-starter. And I left. No harm, no foul, right? But the foolishness of what I did and what could have happened still stays with me.

It may sound silly to say, but all this unwanted attention from men truly unnerved me. Why was it happening? Was I sending out a signal that I wasn't aware of? I thought I was sending out a signal to girls—but if so, then why didn't I attract their advances? Of course, now I understand that I was simply a fourteen-to-fifteen-year-old boy who couldn't really fend for himself yet, which made me a target for all sorts of denizens of the city who wanted to get something for nothing, who wanted to get laid or get paid with minimum hassle. But back then it was confusing, to say the least. And that's why what was going on with Lisa was so important to me. She was such a sweet and genuine person. Everything fit together so well. Sometimes I looked at our bodies as we were having sex, and it was so beautiful, how it all worked. All I wanted for the rest of my life was for everything to work this perfectly, in such unthinking harmony.

My parents had planned a family trip to the Caribbean for the school winter vacation, but I asked them to count me out—I had been to the islands with them a few times already, and I preferred to hang out in the city with friends. Or more specifically with one friend, Lisa, who came to stay with me after my family had left. She stayed for a few days—or was it a week? I truly lost track of time—during which we made love, made food, hung out, pretending to be grownups. But we weren't, and some of the fabric that held us together was starting to fray. Lisa's family was going through a terrible crisis—her older step-brother was claiming that Lisa's mother (his step-mother) had made a pass at him while she was drunk, which she denied—and this was understandably creating huge conflicts for everyone. Lisa wasn't sure what the future might hold, and it was suddenly no longer cool to visit her out there. As for me, my demons were rearing their ugly heads, which meant bad dreams, no sleep and doubts about everything, especially whether I was ready for such a commitment.

* * *

Something happened right before the winter break that had also introduced a note of dissonance into the otherwise harmonious comraderie of the Four Musketeers. Mr Berman had liked something I'd written for the creative writing class, a sonnet; and he had praised it in a way that was designed to make the others feel badly.

"It's the third draft of a poem that will be great after five drafts," he declared to our group. "Shakespeare it ain't, but it is very good, and it's the first thing I've read in here that makes me glad I decided to offer this class. I hope it will serve as a wake-up call for the rest of you."

This is the sonnet, pretty much in the form it was eventually published in *The Manuscript* (I seem to have had a mania back then, probably cribbed from Milton or William Blake, for capitalizing nouns unnecessarily):

> *THE FALL*
> *While drifting in the Firmament of Splendor,*
> *Near sated by the stars' unbounded hymns,*
> *I, soaring on the wings of dream's ascender,*
> *Behold the moon's glory rimmed with lofty whims.*
> *Above, above, in realms of solitude,*

Loose winds arousing in me speedy mirth,
I flourish in majestic quietude
And cast my sullen thoughts upon the earth.
Then suddenly this dream is all afire;
The Nomad's Paradise falls under flame;
And, glaring from the dungeon of desire,
I shake my shackles at alluring fame:
As lonesome as a child unloved by all,
I curse my fate, reflecting on my fall.

It's hard to believe, I know, but no drugs were consumed in the composition of that sonnet. It certainly has "acid trip" written all over it—the grandiosity, the cosmic buzz, the "loose winds" and especially the "speedy mirth." But no, I didn't go that route until a few years later (despite a general feeling at the school, I think, that I was some kind of secret stoner). I achieved this level of abstraction (or pretension, depending on your wont) all on my own, with only the guidance of readings in Milton, Blake, Keats and Giordano Bruno, a Renaissance philosopher who was burned at the stake by the Vatican for heresy, and who was a particular favorite of Mr Berman's. In other words, I was currying favor with the master by using some direct quotes from a sonnet that one of his pet obsessions had written. And apparently it had worked. He had stroked me like a Siamese cat that he had then swung around to attack my buddies with. Yay me.

I had written in my notebook at the time:

Revise, revise. A poem I can revise, but as for my life, I must be content with a first draft, a rough sketching of the master plan. What would be expected, I suppose, following the humble lauding of my work by one so highly regarded, would be an intense joy, a feeling of full delight; yet I felt the opposite. The others in the world seemed so estranged from me.

What I really meant, I think, is that I felt so estranged from them. Instead of doing what a good friend should have—making light of this incident, reassuring them that it really meant nothing—I latched on to it, delighted to have been elevated to the status of teacher's pet.

In so doing, I was laying the groundwork for this "dream's ascender" to indeed become "as lonesome as a child unloved by all." Oh yes, trust me, in very short order I would indeed be "cursing my fate" and "reflecting on my fall."

Chapter 7

THE NOTES THAT I KEPT OF MR BERMAN'S classes make it very clear that I had absolutely no concern about passing any test or getting any particular grade. All I cared about was gaining knowledge, finding answers to the questions that preoccupied me, even tormented me. The fact is, I had lost faith in the beliefs of my parents, I felt like I was drowning, and I needed to find something else to believe in before it was too late. (Or that's how it felt anyway.)

The course offered by Mr Berman in the first semester was titled "*Hamlet* and *Oedipus*," and I guess it was structured around the Ernest Jones book of the same name, which explains Hamlet's famous paralysis of will ("To be or not be") as a manifestation of his "Oedipus Complex." That is, Hamlet wanted to kill his dad and marry his mom, but Claudius (Hamlet's uncle) did this first, so it put Hamlet in a real quandary, since he partly identified with Claudius and even admired him for doing what Hamlet himself did not have the nerve to do. It's one of those psychological analyses that frankly works a lot better in theory than it does in practice, as proven by the Laurence Olivier film version of *Hamlet*, which used the Jones text (which was itself based on an essay that Freud had written, since Jones was Freud's disciple and biographer) as its basis. The film was a big deal when it was released in 1948, winning the Academy Award for Best Picture, and it was still shown a lot in revival houses when I was young, but now you hardly ever see it around. The fact is, reducing Hamlet's dilemma to a diagnosis just seems silly now, laughably so. And Olivier himself is revealed to be what he was at his worst—a runaway ego showing off for the camera, using a classic play as a pretext for displaying his dazzling repertoire of acting tricks. But, again, this kind of Freudian analysis of the mysteries of human (and literary) behavior was all the rage back in the late '40s and '50s; as in Hitchcock's *Spellbound*, which only survives today because its director was—to use Mr Berman's favorite word—a "genius."

Looking over my notes on Berman's class now, his emphasis was less on the psychological than it was on the philosophical concept of Inevitability. Berman called this "the most important concept in Philosophy and in Art." Berman then cited the Roman philosopher Longinus's definition of tragedy, which demands the presence of three situations: (1) The Tragic Hero; (2) The Tragic Situation; (3) Inevitability. He also mentioned George Bernard Shaw's Preface to his play *Saint Joan*, in which Shaw wrote that his tragedy depicted two inevitably opposing forces, both of which were right. That is, Joan of Arc was right to claim that her authority came from God, who spoke to her in a vision; and the Church was right to burn her for saying so, since she was a challenge to their authority and could not be allowed to live unless she recanted. In terms of Shakespeare's *Hamlet*, Hamlet is right in seeking vengeance for his father's death and Claudius is right in trying to protect the state from the threat Hamlet poses; in the end, both of them die.

Berman went on to say that if there is a clear hero and a clear villain, then there can be no tragedy. "Tragic heroes are figures who are somewhat larger than life," Berman stated. That is, these heroes must have "mythic dimension."

This led to a prolonged discussion of the meaning of "myth." According to Berman, "The existence of the phenomena of myths, as well as the particular incidence of myths, is not man-made. They are stories, modes of presenting particular ideas, composed by the culture. The origin of myths is unaccountable. Human beings suffice as the catalysts for myths. But myths themselves are beyond the powers of men to create." Berman added that every culture had a creation myth and that two human actions were universally forbidden—taboo—in every culture: incest and murder.

Mr Berman's conclusion? "Every event in our life is determined by agencies over which we have no control. We are not even deck hands on a sailboat, but instead we think of ourselves as captains." In terms of the character of Oedipus: "Since Oedipus was told that he was going to be the arbiter of such a terrible destiny, why didn't he just go to live in the mountains? Why didn't he take pre-emptive action and kill himself? Why did he marry a woman old enough to be his mother? Because Oedipus was reading from a script his entire life. But what Oedipus had to find out by turning over one page at a time—well, that had already been resolved by the gods. It was impossible for Oedipus to resist or to do anything other than what he did." And Berman ended it all with a quote from Sophocles, the closing lines of *Oedipus the King*: "Count no man happy until he is dead. In death alone is peace."

Yeah, fun times.

I was so bowled over by the breadth of Berman's scholarship and the scope of his lectures that I resolved to get him a holiday/New Year's present to express my gratitude. But what do you get the man who has such a spe-cial affection for death? Then it came to me—buy him something living, something alive! Something that will itself die in a short span of time, thus giving him what seems to make him the happiest! Following this logic, I decided to buy him a plant. But which one? It was an impossible choice. There were so many interesting plants, and all of them were going to die, some sooner, some later. In the end I made a choice.

As I recorded in my notebook at that time:

Jan. 8, 1970. Today I presented Mr Berman with a gift, a wild-leafed begonia, that betokened in a small way the appreciation I felt for being granted the op-portunity of sharing his wealth of knowledge. The begonia's species is a "Nora Belson." Nora embodies for me the fleeting woman, who one views normally only at a distance . . . she's warm yet moody . . . and now she is riding home with me. Mr Berman refused my gift, thwarting the spirit of goodwill in which it was hoped to be received. He felt the petals. He drank of Nora's sweet ambrosia. Then he rebuked her, saying only that he doesn't care for flowers. Yet Nora is a strong woman, and strong women tend to be resilient. . . . Perhaps all is for the best, though. Perhaps I need her love more than Mr Berman seems to. . . .

A few days later, Berman told me to stay after class and meet with him alone. Again, I recorded portions of this meeting in my notebook, something that oddly I would never do again. (To be clear, the following is transcribed from my notebook exactly as I wrote it down right after the meeting took place.)

BERMAN:	*"Sit down, Stephen."*
	(He pressed his arm downward, and I sat.)
BERMAN:	*"Now tell me why you were upset the other day."*
STEPHEN:	*"Oh, you mean the plant. I wasn't so much upset by your refusal as I was disturbed with your unfulfillment of my expectations."*
BERMAN:	*"I didn't like it. I don't want a rancid flower from you, Stephen. I want your soul. I want good poetry. That is the only payment I ask. Why did you get me a gift?"*
STEPHEN:	*"Why did I get you a plant or why did I get you anything?"*
BERMAN:	*"Both."*
STEPHEN:	*"I'll answer the second question first, for that is far simpler."*

(But I didn't write down my answer, as simple as it might have been—I guess that I probably said something about how much his lectures had meant to me, etc. I did, however, record a later part of this same conversation—that is, some connective tissue in the conversation was skipped, and I went instead to the heart of the matter.)

BERMAN: *"Stephen, do you know that you are brilliant? Have you yet realized this? You have a chance to grasp the ungraspable of life and inhabit the furthest-known spheres of our comprehension."*
(He carefully accentuates each word of the following)
"You could be immortal, Stephen. You could. You could. Yet you persist in bandying around your precious gift in ways not worthy of your talent. You may drop this God-given gift of yours, and, though it may seem tough, it is deceptively fragile. And when it shatters, so will you."

STEPHEN: *"I am confused. Why are you telling me this?"*

BERMAN: *"Because I am trying to save your soul, Stephen, impossible though it may seem. There is a very loveable part of you, Stephen. That is your pilgrim soul. It wanders in previously unseen regions of the heart and explores. It works, it sweats, and it's good. There is another part of you, though, that is perverting the nomadic soul. It is your immaturity. You cling to the precipice of childhood, and you are afraid to fall. The fall will be good, Stephen. You will revive and respond in better form than ever."*

[End of recorded scene from notebook.]

I don't recall anything else that may have been said at that time. In fact, I didn't recall this conversation itself until I came across the passages in my notebook, and then, yes, it definitely brought back some memories. For the rest, I remember snippets of several other meetings with Berman, either in his classroom or in the teacher's lounge in the building's basement, in which he murmured similar compliments. I could be the next Charles Dickens, the next Fyodor Dostoievski, if only . . . if only . . . if only I took Mr Berman on as my mentor. If only I put myself in his hands. I do recall him saying: "You will be a good writer no matter what, Stephen. But you cannot be a great writer without my assistance."

As it happened, I was reading *Faust, Part I* in German class at that time (yes, I was taking German, me, a Jewish boy, a mere twenty-five years after the Holocaust; a *schande*, to be sure, but I disliked all the French teachers, and the woman teaching German was cute), and what Berman was saying seemed freakishly close to scenes from Goethe's text. But was he Mephistopheles, trying to snare my soul, or was he trying to save me (as he said)? Could he really help to make me a great writer?

I remember meeting with him once in his classroom with a copy of *Norton's Anthology of English Literature* by his elbow. On the cover were thumbnail photos or sketches of all the great English writers, row upon row of great men (with Virginia Woolf and Edith Sitwell as the lone women). Berman saw me glancing at the pictures. "Do you want to be part of the Pantheon?" he asked.

"Yes," I said. "Yes, I do. More than anything."

"You'll never get there on your own, and you know it," he said.

Yes, he was probably right, I thought. I mean, no one else in my family had even worked in the arts, much less tried to be an artist. I had a great-grandfather who had a store that sold masks for Halloween—that was about as close as I came. So what hope did I really have to make a career in writing, much less make a big impact?

Still, the whole idea of losing control of my life like that, of handing over my power to someone else—even someone as brilliant as Mr Berman—made me nervous.

I went to Mr Cullen and told him the situation. What did he think?

"Well, it's certainly a great opportunity," Mr Cullen said slowly, pondering, slightly squinting at me, as if trying to get the problem in better focus. "Mr Berman is a brilliant scholar and a very good teacher. But if he has a weakness, it's right here," he said, pointing to his heart. "He's all head and very little feeling. If you can keep that in mind, then you should be okay."

I wanted to speak with Mitch, David and Justin about it, but I didn't dare. It would only arouse hostility and resentment. But there was another friend I could talk to, someone who'd had his own dealings with Berman.

Arnold K. was the kind of school friend who I should have been closer to, but somehow it had just never happened. He was fair-skinned, good-looking with blondish-brown hair to his shoulders and a sharp sense of humor. I recall hanging out with him at school dances, scouting the talent. (They bussed girls up to Horace Mann from other private schools for the occasion.) We would smile foolishly, then egg each other on to ask various girls to dance; then afterward we would compare notes or make fun of how awkwardly we executed our steps. He was an excellent tennis player, a smart guy, loads of fun and seemed like the kind of person who had it all. Yet there was a dark side to Arnold, without a doubt, and it came out in the poetry he wrote, several examples of which had been published in *The Manuscript*. Here's one of his that stuck with me.

> *TO WALK IN WINTER IS NOT EASY*
> *By Arnold K.*
> *The trees swayed my path through white woods.*
> *But I'd rather be swayed than chance*
> *The walk on that iced stream that reflected me darkly.*
> *I backtracked, happier to tread old snow.*
> *To walk in winter is not easy.*
> *I can't know how far I didn't go.*

What was eating at Arnold? I could never be sure, but I suspected it may have something to do with Mr Berman. Arnold had been in my *Hamlet* and *Oedipus* class and was in my Milton and Melville classes with Berman this semester. (Maybe in the Renaissance Art History class too, I seem to recall.) But he never spoke in the classes, and I'd seen him have some brief but testy exchanges with Berman. What was that about?

I told him that Berman wanted to take me under his wing.

"Yeah, I figured as much," he said, a dark vein of sarcasm bubbling under the surface. "He always tries to get one or two from each class to join his little club."

"Did he ever try to get you?" I asked.

"I guess. It didn't work out," he told me in a flat voice.

"Well, do you think I should give it a chance?"

"I wouldn't. But do whatever you want to," he said shrugging. "Just watch out. I mean it. Be careful." There seemed to be something else, something more that he wasn't saying. But he had to leave for tennis practice before I could ask him any more questions.

The person who I should have been talking this over with was Lisa, but I couldn't see her right now. Berman had asked me if I had a girlfriend, I told him I did and described my time with Lisa. He told me to break up with her. "You already have so much catching up to do, you can't afford to waste any more time with her," he said.

"But that's not fair," I protested. "You don't even know her."

Berman just shrugged and quoted some lines from *Julius Caesar* to me.

"There is a tide in the affairs of men/which, taken at the flood, leads on to fortune./ Omitted, all the voyage of their lives/ are bound in shallows and in miseries." He looked right at me. "Do you want good fortune or do you want to live in misery?"

Around this time, the Winter issue of *The Manuscript* was published, again including three poems of mine (one of them was *The Fall*, already printed here). The issue was reviewed in *The Record* by Mr Cullen—very odd, since he was also the faculty advisor. Cullen wrote about my work, "These are extraordinary poems . . . It would need another article of at least this length to do justice to them and to their creator; all I can do now is to epitomize an essay in appreciation that must remain unwritten, as follows: at seventeen, Stephen Fife is a more interesting writer than some who have already been awarded the Pulitzer Prize. He is blessed with both a clarity about his art and a modesty about himself that alone would be unusual, but coexisting with a verbal gift that appears to be limitless make his future nothing less than breathtaking to contemplate."

Reading these lines again, at the remove of over forty years, I still wince at the mention of words like "limitless" and "a future that is nothing less than breathtaking to contemplate." I see graveyards full of young poets buried beneath headstones with these words (or similar ones) chiseled on them. I mean, the review was exciting, especially when Cullen compared my work with that of Sam Felder and Nick Vlachos, the two great Horace Mann poets during my years at the school, both of whose bold work had thrilled and inspired me. (Nick Vlachos, who had been my personal idol, later changed his name to Nicholas Christopher and has had a quietly re-markable career as a poet and novelist.) But there are certain times when a review this good is just as bad—or no, maybe it's worse—than a really critical one. At least with a negative review, all your friends try to cheer you up. With a notice this good, no one wants to speak with you, and even your friends can't stand being around you.

Cullen's review had the immediate effect of making me feel that I could never live up to it and would probably never write anything decent again. This was not an unfamiliar feeling. I had grown up with something simi-lar and lived with it for most of my life, having been "the golden boy" of my family who could do no wrong until I started changing in mind and body, upon which I could pretty much do no right. But as a writer I was free—free to fail, free to experiment, free to live, free to choose whatever direction I wanted. At least that's how I felt for a while. But now here I was again, at the same impasse. Feeling like I had to live up to expectations which I could never fulfill.

In the worlds of 2014 or 2004 or 1994—or maybe even 1984, I'm not sure—I would have gone to see the school psychologist, who would have listened to me pour out my troubles and then probably prescribed something to help me deal with them. Something that would lessen my anxiety, something that would decrease this inner tension, this pressure I was putting on myself to live up to an ideal which wasn't even my own. Psychotherapists existed in 1970, of course, and they were mainstream enough that Neil Simon and Mel Brooks and especially Woody Allen could make jokes about them, and everyone in the middle-class audience laughed, familiar with the idea of neurosis and the hapless antics of middle-age neurotics with their panic attacks and sexual problems and sleep issues. But there were no school psychologists that I was aware of—I mean, there probably were some at progressive or experimental schools, but certainly not at a fine upstanding institution like Horace Mann, where mental illness could officially find no quarter. Which is pretty funny when I think back on the school as it was then.

First—out of our graduating class of a hundred or so kids, six committed suicide within six years. Another six to eight eighteen-year-olds had immediate mental breakdowns at Harvard or Yale or Princeton or whatever brilliant institution their tireless efforts at HM had earned them entrance to. Why so many? Well, there was the relentless stress of competition, of course, that white-knuckle terror of not making the cut. Then there was the fact that many kids had problems at home—alcoholism, adultery, divorce, the usual kettle of chaos, but unlike today these were never talked about (yay for Oprah and her descendants!), they were buried in the toxic waste dump of their children's nervous systems, where they blossomed into hideous monsters who chased the children into adulthood. Finally, there was the fact of homosexuality, which at that time was never and could hardly ever be acknowledged. Several of our classmates were gay (a word that didn't even exist then), all of us knew it, and a certain amount of segregating went on, where many of the gay students hung together in an uneasy huddle, while the rest of us ignored them or rarely interacted. I remember one gay student in particular whose face was always covered in angry red pustules—the result, perhaps, of having to exercise so much repression, of having to bury his personality so deeply inside. But no, there were no problems at Horace Mann, everything was Jim-dandy!

Of course, I haven't even talked about the teachers yet—and what a weird, twisted, pathetic, sad-sack bunch many of them were! Not just Tek Young Lin, the pious chaplain, who in 2012 admitted to the *New York Times* that he had sex with several boys during his tenure, and Johannes

Somary, whose blood-chilling crimes have already been mentioned here. The Horace Mann Action Coalition—composed of alumnae who were not themselves molested—have concluded that at least twelve and possibly as many as twenty teachers were physically victimizing students between 1969 and 1999. Just think of that for a moment—somewhere between twelve and twenty predators operating on one campus at the same time, violating some of the 600 students! The chosen ones. How could that be?

One point to consider is that at least a quarter to a third of the teachers were gay, but they had no way of asserting that identity, no way of expressing their personalities, their mode of viewing the world, within the framework that the school offered. The result was a massive amount of personal repression and a habitual concealment of the truth, to the point that up becomes down, black becomes white, and nothing is what it seems. You see what you are supposed to see and you say what you are supposed to say so you can get on with your time there and reap the rewards.

And for many students, this is not a problem, it's simply the way that things are. They go about their business and have a good time and don't pay attention to anything that doesn't concern them. Fine. But it doesn't change the fact that terrible things were going on, things that belonged more to the world of Edgar Allen Poe than anything you'd expect to find at an elite Manhattan prep school.

I should know—I was right in the middle of the mess, and the more I tried to escape it, the more deeply-entrenched I became.

Chapter 8

I AM ALL TOO AWARE (painfully so, believe me) that whatever powers I may have as a writer, they will probably be insufficient to describe the strange charisma and unnerving magnetism that Robert Berman could hold for a student. Though not for every student, of course. As Marc Fisher chronicled in his article about Berman in the April 1, 2013 issue of the *New Yorker* (where he also related some aspects of my story), many were turned off by Berman right away, they found his intensity too threatening or too affected or they simply had no interest in getting that seriously involved in his subjects. According to Marc Fisher, Berman began his first (and only) class that Fisher attended by grabbing a new piece of chalk and drawing a line on top of the blackboard. "This is [John] Milton," he said. Then he drew another line just beneath the first one. "This is Shakespeare." Then he drew two more lines beneath these—"this is Mahler, this is Robert Browning" Finally he threw the chalk on the floor and ground it beneath his black patent leather loafers. "And this is you," he pronounced.

It's a good story, and I suppose it must be true—since Fisher claims he witnessed it—but I never saw anything like it. The Berman I experienced was both more serious than that and more humorous (yes, he did have his own brand of humor), less given to such theatrical displays. But Fisher's story does capture the tenor of Berman's message that prep school students like us, who tested so highly and thought we knew so much, actually knew nothing. There was a world of knowledge about life and human destiny that couldn't be grasped by facile intellects like ours—not yet at least. So be patient, listen well and take notes. And don't try to toss around glib concepts or smartass theories, not in this class—or the full weight of Berman's contempt will come crashing down on you.

This was actually an interesting message for me—interestingly different from anything else I had heard at the school. This teacher took culture seriously—he spoke of it in life and death terms—and he never made any reference to tests or pop quizzes or grades or getting into a prestigious college. That was sweet music to me, I was so sick of the emphasis on college preparation at the school by this point. The world of culture was such a mystery to me—what was driving it, what was it moving toward, what was its purpose? Then again, human behavior seemed very mysterious to me too, especially my own—the conflicting impulses that buffeted me this way and that—how could I be true to myself when I didn't know who that was?

But here was a man, Robert J. Berman, who seemed to know a secret that made sense of it all—and I wanted to find out what that was. This was the source of his appeal for me. He conducted himself with such a sense of certainty, such an absence of self-doubt—whereas I felt so overwhelmed by doubts and insecurities, I often felt like I was drowning in them. Berman seemed stable and solid, a rock in the moving stream that could be held onto while catching one's breath. That's what made him so dangerous.

Berman cultivated a mystique based in part on the lack of any specific details about his own background. From what I'd heard, he had degrees from the University of Michigan and from Yale, he apparently also had a degree in Urdu from the University of Calcutta (or so he said); he also made reference to his having worked as a paleontologist for the Museum of Natural History, to his composing works for the harpsichord and to his making monumental sculptures, but quite honestly it was all very hazy. In fact, everything about Mr Berman—who he was, where he'd come from, what he'd done—was murky and hard to pin down. In one class he'd make a passing reference to having been married to "the greatest woman in the world" whom he'd had a child with, before both mother and child were killed in a horrific car crash in 1957; but then this was never referred to again. He also spoke somewhat vaguely about having been smuggled out of the Soviet Union as a child during the Holocaust—or maybe it was right after the Holocaust. The fact that he was born in 1934 (and yes, that does seem to be a fact) did make that possible. He also referred to having studied with the great Shakespearean scholar G.B. Harrison at the University of Michigan, and others have told me that this was not only true but that there may have been something intimate between them—though this could just be hearsay, and I didn't (and don't) know the truth. Even when I started visiting him in his apartment, I found few if any personal details about his life history that could be gleaned from what I observed.

Now Mr Cullen was a great teacher too, especially when he was working himself into a lather about William Blake's *Songs of Innocence and Experience* or T.S. Eliot's *The Wasteland*. Mr Cullen's background was also a bit mysterious, in that he made passing reference to having studied theology and having been in the advertising business, but nothing very definite about either that I could recall. (He certainly never made reference to being the sole heir to the King Kullen supermarket fortune.) But he did refer to himself several times as "a minor modern poet," and he handed out some examples of his poems. I knew enough by then to be able to admire the quick wit and intelligence they displayed, while also noticing how derivative they were of better poets and how lacking they were in any quality that made them memorable. This helped me to put Mr Cullen into perspective as a man and a teacher, and it contributed to making me feel I could trust him.

Mr Berman, however, never referred to anything specific that he had written (other than his harpsichord pieces), and he certainly never passed anything out to the class. Yet he always gave the sense that he was working on epic projects that would change the world. This oddly magnified Berman's mystique and his appeal. Without any frame of reference to apply to him, we students were at the mercy of his self-mythologizing prowess. Maybe he really was the superior intellect and brilliant philosopher that he appeared to be. He certainly seemed to have read everything ever written (except for modern work, of course, which he "had no use for.")

As opaque as Mr Berman may have been about his personal life and his works, he could not have been more transparent about what he believed. The world, as he viewed it, was divided into "geniuses" and "mediocrities." From what any of us could gather, there was no middle ground, you were either one or the other. The mediocrities had no purpose in life except "to propagate the species" and provide the dross (or raw material) that the geniuses could spin into gold (art or medical/scientific discovery). There was a hierarchy of intellect in world history that measured your worth. The geniuses strode the heights, like the gods in Olympus, and anything they did was interesting just because of their genius, and any act they perpetrated was justified because of their talent. Similarly, they were not subject to analysis as such because their genius was like a prime number—it could not be sub-divided. Genius was what it was; it was *a priori* unique and not subject to the laws and restrictions that governed the rest of humanity. So if the sixteenth century Italian painter Caravaggio killed a man, well, that was okay, because he was a genius; but when Caravaggio died from a mere disease, well, that was a tragedy. And if a mediocrity died, well, that was a cause for celebration, because it freed up some space on a planet already overcrowded with more of the same.

(To borrow the metaphor of Plato's Cave—in which the idea of a thing is real, but the thing itself is merely a shadow of that idea on the cave wall—then, in Berman-world, the geniuses are real, and all other people (the masses of humanity) are merely insubstantial shadows. Or, for those familiar with the David Lean film *The Third Man*, Berman's outlook is not dissimilar from Harry Lime's: "In Italy for thirty years under the Borgias they had warfare, terror, murder and bloodshed, but they produced Michelangelo, Leonardo da Vinci and the Renaissance. In Switzerland they had 500 years of democracy and peace, and what did that produce? The cuckoo clock.")

All of my notes from Berman's lectures—and they were lectures, not discussions like Robin Williams's character initiates in the film *Dead Poets Society*—are studded with the phrase "the great man." "The great man" does this, "the great man" made that happen, "the great man" changed the world. The ultimate expression of this philosophy was Berman's List of *"The 1000 Greatest People Who Have Ever Lived,"* which, for better or worse, I still own. (He actually gave me mine, while he charged others $10 for theirs; whoop-de-do.) At the top of the list, by himself, under the title "Off the Human Scale" is Leonardo da Vinci. The rest of the list is divided into "The First Hundred," "The Second Hundred," etc., and each group of a hundred geniuses is listed in alphabetical order—so as not to hurt the feelings of Buddha, I suppose, when it turned out that he was lower down on the top 100 than Bach. Apparently Berman continues to edit his list to this day, so I can only report on the 1970 version, which has some curious choices, to say the least. So the top hundred (or "The Best of the Best," as he terms it) includes Carlo Crivelli (a decidedly minor early Renaissance Italian painter), Hugo van der Goes (Flemish ditto), Hans Memling (ditto ditto) and Luigi Pirandello, an innovative thinker whose novels have gone stale and whose plays are admired but seldom performed.

Edmund Spenser, who wrote the rarely-read *The Fairy Queen* makes the top hundred, but Walt Whitman only the fifth hundred, Edgar Allen Poe the eighth and Bertold Brecht the tenth. There are women on the list, but very few (I think fourteen in all). The top woman is Virginia Woolf in the third hundred, then comes Sappho in the fourth hundred and Wanda Landowska (harpsichordist) in the fifth; Marie Curie, who discovered radium, sacrificed her life to science and won two Nobel Prizes, only makes the eighth hundred (poor Marie, if only you'd tried a little harder). Oh, I should mention that there is also a "Reserve Collection," for those who weren't quite good enough to make the top 1000. These include Vincent van Gogh, Gauguin, Degas, Cezanne, Kandinsky, Modigliani, Hemingway, Stanislavsky, Henrik Ibsen, George Washington, Pierre Curie (Marie's hubby) and Joan of Arc. (Oh, what a shame, you guys! Maybe next time.) Most of the ladies are in this Reserve Collection (Charlotte Bronte) or else they just managed to sneak into the tenth hundred (Charlotte's sister Emily and *Middlemarch* author George Eliot, who had the good sense to adopt a man's name).

Of course it wasn't hard for those students attracted to Berman's mystique to see the game that was being played. If the choice was between "genius" and "mediocrity," which do you think we wanted to be? Especially since Berman had consigned all our parents *en masse* to the dung-heap of mediocrity. If Berman had been teaching in a college—probably even a community college—then this kind of highbrow rating system would have been subject to a great deal of ridicule, not to mention a slew of complaints from those who felt unfairly judged. But in the small, self-enclosed bubble of Horace Mann School, where students were living at home and hadn't really acquired a strong sense of self yet, it could be very seductive. It certainly seemed so to me. I mean, here was a man with such a huge breadth of scholarship (which he did have) and a fully-functioning system of thought, an ordered hierarchy of the world. Not only that but he wanted to put me—just two years off the swim team!—on the top of that hierarchy without my having to do anything but be myself.

Hot dog! I mean, hey, could it get any better?

Chapter 9

Robert J. Berman loved Renaissance paintings and Renaissance painters the way other people loved family. In fact, he often spoke about them like family members, saying it had been too long since he had seen a particular Michelangelo drawing or Andrea del Sarto painting, and he felt like they had more to say to him. He had a tenderness in his voice when he spoke about paintings that he never had for people. So when he announced that he was going to offer a week-long field trip to Washington, DC over spring vacation, to spend time at the National Gallery and the Phillips Collection, a number of us signed up right away, including all four of the Musketeers.

(Berman's personal credo could, in fact, be found in Walter Pater's conclusion to his landmark book of essays, *The Renaissance, Studies in Art and Poetry*: "Every moment some form grows perfect in hand or face; some tone on the hills or the sea is choicer than the rest; some mood of passion or insight or intellectual excitement is irresistibly real and attractive for us—for that moment only." And, "To burn always with this hard, gem-like flame, to maintain this ecstasy, is success in life.")

It was truly odd and freaky (to use a 1970s word) to go on an outing, a field trip, with Mr B. We met downstairs in Penn Station, the ten students and Berman, and then headed over through the throngs of people to the train platform. The only times I had seen Berman outside of his classroom or the faculty lounge or Cullen's classroom (where the two of them often met) was when he was walking (usually with Mr Cullen) across the school grounds to the teachers' lunchroom. I had never seen him on the 242nd Street subway platform, as I had several other teachers, never seen him walking up or down the hill, never seen him walking out of Central Park (as I had seen Mr Evans the French teacher, dressed all in leather). But here we were in this most public of places, Penn Station, out among the populace. It was beyond surreal, seeing Berman in this setting. And then came one of those touches that was almost too perfect, that makes one feel as if life really might be a Hollywood movie.

A group of four young African-American men in their late teens or early twenties began singing the Temptations' song *My Girl*, a true urban rhapsody and Motown classic (even back then). It was one of my favorite songs and one that I had many associations with already, with various girlfriends. But there may have been no one in the world who was less Motown, less Rhythm & Blues, than Robert Berman. The sinuous hooks and lush harmonies only made him wince with pain, and he hurried us through the bustling station, somehow managing to resist putting his hands over his ears.

Once in DC, we quickly made our way to the hotel, which as I recall was rather brown, drab and nondescript. Nevertheless many of my fellow students wanted to go off and explore our new surroundings. I wasn't interested and started unpacking my things and putting them in the bureau drawers. I can't recall who I was rooming with, but whoever it was had gone off with the others, leaving me alone in the room. I was completely caught up in the task at hand when someone came up behind me and whirled me around. I had a very quick glimpse of Mr Berman's face and his black-framed glasses as he tipped me slightly off-balance and thrust his tongue down my throat. I suddenly felt like I was drowning—his tongue was muscular and aggressive, it seemed to have a life of its own as Berman held me off-balance in a classic dance dip, as if we were in the middle of some kind of ballroom dance contest. I struggled to regain my balance and push him off, but it was difficult to get any traction. I felt him put a hand down my pants and touch my butt-crack. I tried to protest, but it was impossible to get any words out with his tongue clogging my mouth. I heard him breathing heavily, which was somehow the most horrifying sound I can ever remember hearing. He was wearing some kind of musky after-shave, a very strong scent, but I instinctively tried not to smell it, as if that was simply more reality than I could stand. And still his tongue thrust itself into the orifice of my throat like an invasive animal on a mission.

He tried to shift my body's position so I would fall on the bed, and it was in that moment that I was finally able to regain my balance enough to push him off. I scrambled to get to my feet and stood a few feet away, staring at him in disbelief. He was wearing a gray button-down shirt with the top two buttons undone and charcoal-gray slacks. His heavy breathing was becoming normal again, thank God. He always seemed bigger in his classroom, but now he looked small and slight, smaller than ever.

"What are you doing?" I asked, barely able to form the words.

"Only what you wanted me to," he answered, looking me in the eyes.

"I don't," I said. "I don't want that."

"Then you don't know yourself well enough to know what you want," he said, not backing down.

"You're wrong," I said.

"You sent out a signal, and I responded, that's all," he told me.

"I didn't. You're mistaken. You—You—"

But I couldn't talk anymore. The adrenaline was shutting down and the shock kicking in. I walked out of the room and into the carpeted hallway, then I walked down the stairs and into the lobby, where I took a seat.

How could that have happened?

How could that have happened?

No, really—how could that have happened?

I couldn't have been more shocked if a UFO had landed in the room and a small visitor from another planet had emerged.

This wasn't the early 2000s with *Queer as Folk* playing on Showtime and popular culture embracing "the gay lifestyle." It wasn't even the late 1970s with Donna Summer singing disco at Studio 54. It was 1970, and my frame of reference just didn't encompass an event such as this.

Then again, maybe it didn't matter what year it was, maybe the act of a respected teacher sticking his tongue down my throat, violating me that way, would have been shocking whenever it happened.

But what should I do?

What could I do?

How could this have happened?

* * *

I didn't tell anyone.

I couldn't tell anyone—there were no words to describe it. Or if there were, then I couldn't say them.

I had my best friends, my three fellow Musketeers with me, and I couldn't tell them. I didn't even think about doing so.

Did I send out a message to Mr Berman that I wasn't aware of?

I wasn't aware of doing so, but maybe I was wrong. Maybe he was right, and I just didn't know myself. Maybe I was wrong about everything.

How could that have happened?

Did that even happen?

What happened?

Mr Berman said nothing more about it.

He didn't mention it for the rest of the trip and behaved as if it had never happened.

Did it? Did it happen?

It did. Of course it did. I could still taste his tongue in my mouth, a salty, scratchy taste, it made me want to vomit.

But it still didn't make any sense. How could it have happened?

I walked through the museum with my friends and Mr Berman, gazing at all the paintings that I'd been so excited to see. But I didn't feel anything. I couldn't really see them. I started to get angry at myself and mentally beat myself up. Just look at the paintings! Stop being so distracted! What's wrong with you?

What's the big deal anyway? So he put his tongue down your throat? It's not the end of the world. It's not like he did any physical damage. What's the big deal?

But it was the shock of it. The shock. The fact that he caught me off-guard, put me off-balance, that he came up behind me, that I didn't even see him before it happened, that I didn't know it was coming, and then when it happened, I lost my balance, and he put his hand down my pants, and I couldn't defend myself, and I didn't have any say, and then it was too late, it had happened, and now there was no way I could forget it. There was no way I could take it away. No way I could undo it.

It had happened, and I couldn't go back. I couldn't un-remember it, no matter how hard I tried. And I did try.

The thing is, I didn't expect it. Hadn't expected it. He caught me off-guard.

But did it happen?

* * *

Two weeks later, back at school, Mr Berman asked me to stay after class.

"I think I may have been wrong about you," he said.

"What?" I asked.

"I think we shouldn't meet again for a while," he told me.

"What do you mean?" I asked.

"I think we need to take a step back and not meet for a while. Then, if we come back together, we'll move on from there. And if we don't, then we won't."

"I feel like you're punishing me," I said, "like I did something wrong."

"No, I'm just saying that this isn't working out as I'd hoped. And I don't think it's helping you. So let's just take a hiatus and see what happens."

What I wanted to say was "What about all those things you said, about how I couldn't be a great writer without your help? What about that?"

But I didn't. I just got up and left.

Chapter 10

WHEN MITCH BRONFMAN and I were at the Model United Nations representing Bulgaria—and before we'd gotten thrown out of the negotiations for throwing chicken bones at the Soviet Union—we had heard about some truly incredible student travel deals to Europe and in Europe for the following summer. Like $194 roundtrip from New York to London! And $27 from Dublin to Paris! And then a student Eurail pass was like $60! For the whole month!

It was then that Mitch and I came up with the idea of going to Europe together for the summer. His dad had invited Mitch to come stay with him in London when the school year was over. His dad was loaded, with a huge house in some swanky section of London—so of course there wouldn't be any problem in him putting me up too! And then we could pal around that old continent together, going to museums, seeing paintings, taking in all the sights and picking up Euro-girls! How cool was that?

Mitch's mom and two dads signed off on the idea pretty swiftly, as long as I was going to be along for the ride. My parents weren't nearly as receptive.

"Why can't you go as part of a youth tour?" they asked.

"Because there are no youth tours that go where we want to go!" I answered impatiently.

"Where do you want to go that's so off the beaten track?" my mom asked.

"Colmar! There are no youth tours that go to Colmar, and I absolutely have to go."

"Why?" my mom asked.

"Where is Colmar? I never heard of it," my dad put in while reading the Sports section of the *New York Times*.

"It's in the south of France. That's where the Issenheim Altarpiece is! By Matthias Grunewald!"

"Who?" my mom asked.

"The what?" my dad asked.

"The Issenheim Altarpiece is only one of the greatest works of art in the entire world," I practically shouted, then threw in: "And youth groups do not go where the Crivellis and the van der Goes paintings are!" (At that time I was still taking Berman's recommendations on faith.)

"The who?" my mom asked.

"The what?" my dad asked again.

"Oh, what's the use?" I wailed, throwing my hands up and leaving the room.

This exchange took place over a month *before* the trip to DC. The idea that I was going to Europe with a friend my age (actually eleven months younger) to see a lot of Christian-themed paintings did not sit well with my parents. The previous summer they had made arrangements to send me to Israel to live on a kibbutz for two months when they panicked, worried that another war might break out in the Middle East, and I would be caught in the middle. So instead I went to the social work camp in Kentucky, where I got arrested at Fort Knox and thrown into the brig. Actually my mom was completely okay with that, in fact she was more than okay. All four of us who were arrested there had to get permission from our parents before the army would agree to release us. The parents of my three friends (my buddy Todd and two strong-spirited girls, both wearing tank tops and shorts and sandals) were appalled when they received the calls, and they had apologized profusely for their children's wrong-headedness. In my case, the stormtrooper—I mean, military policeman—had come back, looking befuddled. "What's wrong with your mom? She cheered when I told her where you were. She said that I'd made her day."

This going to Europe with Mitch for three months was something else, though. The airfare and train deals were certainly outstanding, and they admired the independence it showed, but this lack of adult supervision was giving them pause. Who would we even call if something went wrong? Who would be our emergency contact?

"Mitch's dad is our emergency contact," I told my mom. "He's right there in London. He has loads of money, and he isn't tied down to a job, so he could come help us out of any jam."

This was better than nothing, but it didn't make my mom feel that much better either. She didn't know Mitch's dad, wasn't in touch with him. He was an Independent Producer, which wasn't a very reassuring job to have for an emergency contact. Then my mom remembered that her friend Jimmy Breslin was going to be over in Dublin with his family for the summer. Breslin—the renowned *Daily News* columnist who had just finished running an unsuccessful but highly amusing campaign for Lieutenant-Mayor of New York City on Norman Mailer's ticket—was fine with Mitch and me staying at his house in Dublin after we left London. And he agreed to be my emergency contact during my trip. So that was it then. Mitch and I had all the permissions we needed, and soon we had the money as well. We gleefully went down to the Student Travel Bureau (or whatever it was officially called—very sad that it no longer exists!) and purchased our tickets to paradise.

But again, all this took place before the trip to DC, which, needless to say (but I'll do so anyway), had shaken me to the core.

For a brief moment after leaving Berman's classroom (following the start of our personal "hiatus"), I was so furious that I wanted nothing more to do with anything connected with him, including my trip to Europe with Mitch. But the next moment that trip meant more to me than ever. It was something solid in my future, something I could count on, something I was looking forward to, something that Berman couldn't ruin. Mitch and I had become closer than ever, we felt like spiritual brothers—planning out the route we would take and the paintings we would see on the way—and boy, did I ever need that right then!

I was happy also to have Mr Cullen there to fill the void that Berman had left behind. Where Berman was all about the worship of dead "geniuses" and their creations, Cullen made us aware of Zen Buddhism and the life of the spirit. He told Mitch and me (we were in the same class with Cullen) to study the book *Zen in English Literature and Oriental Classics* by the English author R.H. Blythe. This volume—which locates the essential aspects of Zen in the great works of both Western and Eastern Literature— soon grabbed my attention with quotes like: "Zen, though far from indefinite, is by definition indefinable, because it is the active principle of life itself." Soon this became my handbook which I carried everywhere, providing wisdom and a great deal of solace. (It's still a book I truly admire.)

A few weeks after the break from Berman, I was asked by Mr Cullen to stay after class. When I did, he said he had a funny story about the previous evening's "parent/teacher night" to tell me.

"Your parents were there," he said, "and I went over to them and took them aside and said, 'You know that your son is a genius, don't you?' And your mother just looked at me strangely and said, "Are you sure you have the right parents?'"

I didn't react, which I guess irked Mr Cullen.

"Come on now, that's odd, to say the least," Mr Cullen remarked. "I've read so many Jewish short stories, by Bellows and Philip Roth and Bernard Malamud—the Jewish mothers always think their children are geniuses, no matter how little talent they really have. But here I say that you really are one, and your mother doesn't believe me."

Yes, got it. And it made me unhappy on two counts—first, that my mom couldn't even come up with something diplomatic to say. (After all, she was a politician.) And then there was that word again—"genius." It was a Berman word that I'd grown tired of hearing. I was still trying to shake the effects of Cullen's rave review of my poems, which had made it more difficult for me to write, causing me to become even more self-conscious. I think this comes through all too clearly (even in the abbreviated form presented here) in an essay I wrote for Cullen at the time.

REALITY AND FANTASY

Part I

I am torn between the real and the unreal. I drift through the streets and alleys of New York, and I wish to be gone like a feather in the wind. I desire my freedom so greatly that at times the need to escape this desolate existence overwhelms me.

While I am here I often dwell in a world of fantasy. My ambitions, though, reach further into life than even my wildest dreams can imagine. I seek a spiritual happiness that is denied to most who seek it. I envision this spiritual awareness as a radiant palace towering above both town and country, somewhere in the region of the moon and stars, where a sense of peacefulness and ease prevails.

I have aspirations to be a poet, a dramatist; I often wonder why. I suppose the reason lies in the fact that there is so much man must learn in this world, and every bit of knowledge discovered narrows the distance between earth and heaven. Possibly through my writing there can be a communion between nature and the soul of man.

My soul is restless; my entire being is like an imprisoned cat who awaits the day when the door of his cage will be flung open. Though the ways of men appear strange and violent to me, I wish to know and understand people from every walk of life.

The horizons of the world appear unbounded; I look forward to the day when man and the city will not seem so strange and unnatural to me.

Part 2

Envision for a moment a sea of up-curled waves on which floats a fleet of sailing vessels. All the boats are swaying with the whimsy of the breeze, their canvas sails waiting for a sudden gust of wind. The wooden crafts are drifting apparently without direction, and many boats appear to be colliding, seriously impairing any prospects for a long voyage. Yet aside from the various shades of weatherworn paint, all the boats appear to be basically the same. To complete the picture, the sun is either rising or setting on the distant horizon, and the clouds are wandering listlessly along the placid horizon.

And where am I, the artist, in this picture?

I am steering a craft that seems as directionless as the fleet; this boat floats alone, possessing within its hull the stillness of the sea. My boat, though similar to every other boat, is, to the discerning eye, distinguishable from its brothers, for each vessel transports a different cargo. The cargo of my boat does not glitter beneath the radiance of the sun's golden eye, and I would want it to be so. I have just begun to dig beneath the outer layer of dust, and my senses assure me that there must be a treasure hidden underneath.

I am learning to have faith in the little puff of wind that may allow me to survive the imminent storm. Though the winds may blow with all heaven's fury, thus wiping out the progress that I appear to have made, I must drift within Reality's wake and retain the memory of my dream emblazoned upon the horizon. Though the waves may toss me at their mercy like a giant rolling me down his arm in jest, my boat will face toward the sanctuary on the unknown sea where the men who have attained heaven within themselves abide.

But is the sun rising or setting? This depends on who beholds the scene.

In my eyes, presently, the sun is rising; the first golden arrow has sprung from the crossbow of the celestial archer. Though the waves have been becalmed and the waters hold me as if at anchor, I feel a certain turbulence in the air that foretells of coming changes.

* * *

I was still angry at the way that Berman had treated me, and the more I thought about it, the angrier I got. How dare he bring me so close to him with all that praise, then push me away! How dare he sneak up on me and kiss me like that, then say it was somehow my fault! How dare he toy with my affections like that!

These thoughts swirled around in my mind day and night until I couldn't think about anything else and had trouble sleeping. If only I could tell someone I knew! But I was still too confused and embarrassed to do that. Instead I decided to lodge a complaint directly with the school, and I went to the office of Dr Philip Lewerth, Associate Headmaster.

Why did I choose to tell Dr Lewerth? To be completely honest, I can't recall the reasoning that led me to make this decision. The head of the school at that time was Dr Harry Williams, formerly the head of the

Science Department, who I didn't feel especially close to. The Guidance Counselor (and head of the History Department) was Dr William Clinton, a large bear-like man who had always intimidated me. So I guess that Dr Lewerth seemed like my best option. He was a down-to-earth man, a "straight shooter" who must have seemed like someone who would take seriously what I told him.

I met with Dr Lewerth in his office in April 1970. I told him that something had happened on the recent spring vacation field trip to Washington DC, something very upsetting: Mr Berman had touched me in a sexual way.

"How exactly do you mean?" Dr Lewerth asked.

"Just what I said—he did something sexual. That's all I want to say right now."

"Did anyone see this happen?" Dr Lewerth asked.

"No."

"Do you have any hard evidence to support what you have told me?" Dr Lewerth asked.

"No."

"Is there anything else you can offer in the way of corroboration?" Dr Lewerth asked.

"No, there isn't."

"I see. What would you like to happen now?" Dr Lewerth asked.

I hesitated. "I'd like you to call Mr Berman into your office with me present, so I can ask him if he did what I said."

Now it was Dr Lewerth's turn to hesitate. Then he told me, "Sorry, but I don't see that happening."

"Why not?" I asked.

Then Dr Lewerth told me that it was Horace Mann's Sexual Abuse policy to favor the teacher unless there was compelling evidence against him.

"But that's not fair," I said.

"Well, that's our policy," Dr Lewerth told me. Then he added: "My advice to you is simply to drop it."

This was too frustrating to bear. It had been so difficult for me to work up the nerve to come in here, and now he was just turning me away!

"Why can't you just call him in here and ask him yourself?" I asked. I wanted Mr Berman to know that he couldn't build me up with so many promises and then just walk away.

"I'm going to be straight with you, Mr Fife," Dr Lewerth told me. "Any complaint against Mr Berman would have to go through Dr Clinton. Mr Berman has strong supporters at the school, and Dr Clinton is one of them. So I don't recommend that you go any further with your complaint. Do we understand each other?"

I didn't move. I hadn't expected this. I wasn't happy.

"If you want, I could make Dr Clinton aware of your complaint, and we can see what he says. But I'm telling you right now that I don't recommend this."

"Yes, go ahead, tell him," I said. I felt desperate, there was no way I could work up the strength to do this again. I felt deprived, I wanted to have something to show for all my efforts.

"If you insist," Dr Lewerth said. "But here's something else to think about. If you go public with your charge, then Mr Berman would have the right to sue you for libel."

"What?" I asked.

"Your parents might have to pay damages," he added.

"Really? Why would my parents have to be involved?"

"Because you're a minor," Dr Lewerth said. "The court would compel them to pay any damages that might be incurred."

"That doesn't seem fair," I said again.

"I'll let you know when Dr Clinton has issued a response," Dr Lewerth told me, then ushered me out of his office.

Over the next two weeks I was tormented by doubt, guilt and hope—doubt that I had done the right thing in going to Lewerth, guilt that I may have "betrayed" Mr Berman and hope (equally) that I would be believed and that I wouldn't be. After what had happened to me with Mr Lin (the ear-tugging), it meant so much to me that I be taken seriously now and not treated as the powerless pawn that I'd been back then. But I also didn't want Mr Berman to be fired. I just wanted him to be censured for violating my boundaries and to have him know that these must be respected. That is, *I* demanded respect. Then maybe Mr Berman and I could reach a new agreement.

While I was waiting to hear back from Lewerth, I called Lisa, who I hadn't seen for a while. She came into the city that Saturday, which was a lovely spring day, one of those perfect days, a bottomless beaker of sweetness.

Lisa and I walked through Central Park hand-in-hand, and the old sense of our being made for each other came rushing back. We sat on a big rock overlooking the Central Park pond, hugging and kissing, wondering why we had spent so much time apart. Her shoulder-length dark hair, her pale skin, her cherry-red lips—I saw them as in a dream, I was drunk on them, blissfully drunk. The day slipped by slowly, and I never wanted it to be over. Finally, though, we had to leave.

We were taking the subway to Grand Central Station when something odd happened. Four slender men from India sat down on the opposite row of seats, facing where I was sitting with my arm around Lisa. She was wearing a thin summer dress, and the men began staring fixedly between her legs as if she had a TV set there, showing their favorite program. Then two of the men started touching their genitals and rhythmically masturbating, big smiles on their faces. Lisa didn't notice, but I was upset and very angry. I wanted to smash those smiles off their faces, but I also knew they'd just deny what they were obviously doing. So I whispered to Lisa to stand up and walk with me to the other end of the car. She gave me a confused look but did what I'd asked. I looked back and saw the men laughing, their heads bunched together, enjoying their joke.

We got to Lisa's family's home in Westchester around 7:00 PM and had dinner with her parents and some of her brothers and sisters. There was an attempt to make amusing small talk, but a tension was underneath things, a palpable tension, and everything came out sounding wrong. In fact, oddly, everything seemed to have become wrong since that masturbation incident on the subway.

Well, no, that wasn't true. On the train Lisa had fallen asleep with her head on my shoulder, and that was really sweet, I had kissed her ear through her dark locks and shed a tear because I felt so close to her then. But all that was suddenly gone and everything seemed cold and ugly now. I looked at Lisa and saw only that her jaw seemed too big and her hair seemed too low on her forehead. Everything she said sounded stupid. I kept reminding myself that this was the woman I'd felt so close to just a few hours ago. But I suddenly found myself hating her.

Was it because I was looking at her with Berman's eyes?

It's true that his calling her a "time-waster" kept coming back into my mind, but maybe this was just an excuse, maybe I was just immature. Maybe I just didn't deserve her. In any case, the more immediate problem was what to do next? Our plan was to go to bed separately then meet in the playroom, as per our established routine. But all I wanted to do now was get out of there, run through the woods to the train station, jump on the train and end up back home.

I didn't, of course. (The trains weren't running at that hour anyway.) I got out of bed, made my way through the alternating rectangles of light and shadow to the playroom, where Lisa was waiting in her white nightie and white panties. I could see her breasts through the fabric, her dark-red nipples large and erect. I tried (not very successfully) not to think about the four Indian men on the subway who seemed to view Lisa as their own private peep show. Lisa and I made love, but it was tense, not relaxed; it was humorless and emotionless; and it was over in a matter of minutes, much quicker and more perfunctory than usual.

"That was nice," Lisa cooed sweetly, smiling at me. "Did you like it?"

"Yeah, sure," I said, trying to smile back.

"Me too," Lisa whispered, then she fell asleep in my arms, her head on my shoulder.

I didn't sleep all night. I lay there stiffly, stone cold awake. Lisa snored quietly, I'd never noticed that before. It bothered me—but suddenly everything did. My shoulder fell asleep; it was the only part of me that would. I didn't want to move and wake up Lisa. But around 5:00 AM, as the first rays of light were appearing, I moved my shoulder and woke Lisa up and told her we needed to go back to our rooms. She nodded sleepily, kissed me quickly and went back to her bedroom. I returned to the guest room, where I finally nodded off.

A few hours later, Lisa knocked on the door. We had a quick breakfast, then she drove me to the train station.

We had around ten minutes before the train was scheduled to arrive.

"I had a great time," she told me sweetly with a big smile.

I didn't say anything.

"Didn't you?" she asked.

"I don't think this is working anymore," I told her.

"What?' she replied, startled.

It wasn't what I had wanted to say, and I wanted so badly to take the words back. But I couldn't. And Lisa was weeping—softly at first, then a cloudburst of tears. And the more she wept, the more hard-hearted I became, until it felt like I was several miles away, looking down at her.

"You said you loved me," she cried, the tears streaming down.

"I did," I said, "I do."

"Well, what happened?" she practically screamed.

I didn't know. It was like Lisa was a crystal clear pond that Berman's contempt had polluted. I couldn't seem to get past the judgment he had pronounced, no matter how hard I tried. Everything was simple, spontaneous, unthinking before; now I was thinking too much, not feeling enough. And nothing felt right. There didn't seem to be anything I could do about it except pray a little harder that the train would show up.

And finally it did.

I gazed at Lisa from a window seat as the train pulled away, watching her wipe the tears away and put the car in reverse.

"I'll see her again sometime soon," I thought to myself, "this can't be the end."

But I knew in my heart that it was.

A few days later, I got a note to come down to Dr Lewerth's office.

"Dr Clinton urges you not to make your complaint public," Lewerth said sternly. "You need to consider the gravity of the charges. You would only tarnish yourself."

"You won't even question Mr Berman?" I asked.

Dr Lewerth shook his head. "And if you file a complaint against him, then the school will come down on his side. And you may do irreparable damage to your future."

That didn't worry me nearly as much as the prospect of everyone (including my parents) finding out about that kiss. Or my having to tell that story aloud to the world.

I melted into tiny beads of sweat at the thought. Tiny beads that evaporated into the air, becoming as nothing.

Chapter 11

MITCH BRONFMAN AND I WERE SPENDING all our spare time plotting out our route across Europe as if we were explorers with dreams of discovering a new land. Well, it was new to me anyway—I had never been to London or Paris or anywhere in Europe. And I was deliriously happy at the prospect of so much freedom! An entire continent that didn't know me and that I didn't know! And Mitch and I were going to explore it together! I unfolded the map with all its brightly-colored squares and its names that held no associations for me, and I filled it up with heroic poems about valiant acts of derring-do that Mitch and I were going to perform. I had no idea what these acts might be, but I knew they were going to be stellar and original and . . . not boring. Starting with a week with Mitch's celebrity dad, who lived in splendor in a huge house in Eton Square (loved that!) and completely unlike my dad or any other dad I had ever known. Or so I hoped.

In the last week of school—and just five days before we were scheduled to leave—Mr Berman asked me to meet with him. Berman and I hadn't spoken outside of class since his pronouncement of our hiatus. My anger at him had waned a bit, though I was still deeply weirded-out by that kiss.

"What are your plans for the summer, Mr Fife?" Berman asked me.

I told him about my travel plans with Mitch. I tried to sound cool and detached, but I couldn't keep the excitement I was feeling from leaking into my tone.

"I want you to cancel your plans and stay here with me in New York for the summer," he said.

"What?" I asked.

"You heard me," he said.

I hadn't necessarily expected him to share my excitement, but I thought he'd be at least a little bit proud that Mitch and I were going to so many museums and churches that he had recommended.

"But we've brought our tickets already," I told him. "We've made arrangements. We have places to stay."

He didn't answer.

"Why would I do that?" I asked.

"Because I'm making you an exceptional offer," he said with deep seriousness. "One that will not be repeated."

I didn't hesitate in my response.

"No," I said. "I won't do it."

"Then you are a fool, Mr Fife," he said. "You are a fool."

Mr Berman stood up and left the room.

I sat there, feeling suddenly heavy and weighted down.

* * *

That first week in London was everything I had looked forward to and more.

The London National Gallery, the British Museum, the Victoria and Albert, the Courtland Institute, even the Tate—wow! Holbein, Velazquez, Raphael, Michelangelo, Van Eyck, Botticelli, Caravaggio, Rembrandt, Leonardo da Vinci, Shakespeare Quartos, the Elgin Marbles, the British Empire—double wow! This was the real thing, this was *culture*. This was the world that Berman had opened the door to, and I felt like I had walked through into an endless vista of beauty and truth. Mitch and I went to Westminster Abbey and recited poetry over the graves of Browning, Chaucer and Tennyson. We went to St. Paul's Cathedral and marveled at that architectural miracle. In fact, all of central London seemed like a miracle—the impossible green of Hyde Park, the twisting streets out of Dickens and Thackeray, the English "birds" in their mod miniskirts and eager smiles. (And the dollar was strong and the pound was weak and everything was so cheap!)

Louis Bronfman (not his real name), Mitch's dad, was a larger-than-life character, a man made to portray a featured character in a Philip Roth novel—a self-made Jew living a glamorously eccentric life in the exclusive heart of a deeply anti-Semitic city, a man in his fifties who was focused to an almost obsessive degree on his own libidinal pleasures. As it turned out—though of course we didn't have a clue at the time—this was his heyday, when he produced successful movies for the British film industry and successful plays for the West End and Broadway. The future would prove a long downward spiral for Lou, a streetcar named Desire to nowhere, but right now he was living like a lord in Eton Square, with a blond mistress who was one of the most beautiful women I had ever seen, much less eaten strawberries and cream with. Oddly—and this was indeed odd—when Mitch and I arrived, his dad had us stay in this mistress's flat and moved her into his enormous townhouse a few blocks away.

Wouldn't it have made more sense to have Mitch—his older son, whom he rarely saw—installed in one of the magnificent townhouse's many rooms and leave the mistress out of the immediate equation? (I certainly thought so at the time, but I didn't say anything to Mitch, who was already unhappy with the situation.) Instead Mitch and I had to make do in the small flat and sleep together in the one bed, only going over to the townhouse in the evenings or on the weekend. When we were there, Lou Bronfman and his Austrian mistress proved to be charming, witty people who enjoyed each other's company and tolerated ours. Their dinner conversation was peppered with references to British dramatists and actors like "Terry" Rattigan and Harold Pinter and "Larry" Olivier, names that meant little or nothing to me at the time. I remember sitting with Lou and his mistress (whom he did eventually marry, then divorce) and watching a World Cup soccer match, which they were all worked up about, but which bored Mitch and me to tears. How could such a celebrated and glamorous personage sit around for hours watching "football," as they insisted on calling it?

I could see Mitch getting more frustrated and upset as the week wore on. This certainly wasn't the father-son reunion that he had hoped for.

Not surprisingly, the anger that Mitch felt about how things were turning out with his dad carried over into his and my friendship. There was always an underlying dynamic between us in which he would become more distant and critical with me, which would then make me more insecure and self-conscious and would end up leading to arguments between us, usually over silly or petty things like the way I pronounced a painter's name or the sound of my laugh ("you laugh like a hyena!" he'd grumble) or the awkward way I could be around pretty girls.

The more shut off Mitch became emotionally, the more commanding he was with girls, who just seemed bowled over by his cruel indifference (the crueler, the better). The fact that he was almost a year younger than me really stung and further eroded my self-confidence.

Still, those ten days in London were mostly a joyous blur of visits to museums and cultural institutions and walks down twisting roads that often led to wonderful places. It was a little weird sleeping in the same bed with Mitch—even with my own brothers, that had never happened—but it also wasn't that big a deal (as it always seems to be in American sitcoms—the level of homosexual panic for straight guys just seems off the charts!). When I felt close with Mitch, it was truly like having a brother by my side, a soul brother, someone I could trust absolutely. When we'd been arguing, though, then I couldn't get far enough away from him (or him from me). But Mitch is still the closest male friend I've ever had, and the odd circumstance that threw us together like that remains a fond memory.

We moved on to Oxford, Wales and Dublin, accumulating experiences and ever-fiercer disagreements. Jimmy Breslin offered to take us with him to Belfast to witness "The Troubles" between the Catholics and Protestants up close; but we opted instead to stay with Breslin's enormous family (his first wife, their several children and the children's friends) and hang out at James Joyce's tower. Then we took a student flight to Paris, where we stayed together in in a small bed-and-breakfast for a few days. The arguments between us had become so intense, we both said things we shouldn't have and couldn't take back. And then our destructive dynamic would assert itself: he would become cold and cruel, I would be pathetically plaintive and needy. We finally agreed to split up.

This was only three weeks into our three month trip—so I spent the next two-plus months on my own, going from city to city, from museum to museum, following the route that Mitch and I had planned out. But of course Mitch was following the same basic route, so we would run into each other in various galleries or bed-and-breakfasts. Or not.

A definite highlight was meeting up with Mitch in front of Grunewald's Issenheim Altarpiece in Colmar, France. Mr Berman was right about this one, a soaring, cosmic painting, a mind-bending vision of the tragedy and triumph of the human spirit—made even better when the man at the bed-and-breakfast thought Mitch and me were twins. He couldn't believe that we weren't even related. Mitch and I had dinner together, and I thought for an evening that we could patch up our differences. But then he left in the morning, and I spent more time communing with the Grunewald paintings, a Jewish guy from New York City hanging out for hours with a blond Christ.

In Madrid, Mitch and I ended up sharing an enormous room together near the Prado Museum that was only $2/day. (This was at the tail end of the rule of General Francisco Franco, whose martial law had kept prices insanely low.) Then I went off to Ibiza, where (unbeknownst to me) Mitch was watching me step off the ferry from a café verandah. He was sitting with a local girl who he then took to bed, while I took a bus to the other side of the island, re-reading *Zen in English Literature and Oriental Classics* while sharing an isolated beach with a bunch of fat, naked Germans.

We met up one last time in Florence, Italy in late July. Mitch had rented a room in a converted convent near the Uffizi Gallery—he had an uncanny ability to find the best rooms anywhere at the lowest prices. He was leaving for a week on a tour of neighboring towns, so he offered to let me stay in the room while he was gone. It felt like a safe haven after all the loneliness and depression I'd been feeling for the past month of days and nights on my own. Berman's voice echoing: "You are a fool, Mr Fife"—that followed me from town to town, from museum to museum, from bed to bed that I couldn't fall asleep in. The only thing that kept me sane was writing letters to Mr Cullen, describing all the places I'd seen, all the ways I was changing—"for the better," I wrote, even though it didn't really feel that way. But now, staying in this bare convent room in the heart of the world's most cultured city, it felt like I was getting some of myself back again, like maybe the Truth that accompanied Beauty wasn't all bad.

Then Mitch returned, and things didn't go well between us. He was broke, and he thought up all sorts of reasons why I owed him money. I gave him a small sum, but he wanted more, and I wouldn't fork it over. Our final showdown came in the middle of the night on a dark street amid all the objects of architectural beauty.

As I recorded in my notebook later that day, Mitch sneered at me, "Everything you do arouses hatred in me. Things that I could stand in any other person I can't tolerate in you. To tell you the truth, there is no one in the world I'd less like to be with."

That took all the fight out of me, I started crying. That's when he told me how much he'd love to kill me, how he had vivid fantasies of doing so. Then he walked away, leaving me weeping like a fool (that word again!) in the public square.

"I wonder what could inspire such animosity in him toward me," I wrote in my notebook, but I understand now how much it had to with the ferocity of the anger he felt toward his father, and the fact that we were sixteen- and seventeen-years-old respectively, not nearly mature enough to handle the emotional consequences of spending three months in a foreign continent on our own. He dealt with his pain by directing it outward toward others. I dealt with mine by directing it inside at myself, something I seemed to have a nearly infinite capacity for. That dynamic between us—not a good mix. Nearly fatal, in fact.

A few weeks later, I stayed up all night in Rome before my flight back to Manhattan.

At 4:00 AM, I snuck past the guard ("O three-headed Cerberus!") into Palatine Hill and lay down among the ancient Roman graves. It was cool and dark and peaceful. There was nothing to fear, no one who would hurt me here.

I distinctly remember how deeply I envied the dead.

Chapter 12
Ghosts in the Poet's House

IT ALL STARTED WITH *PREP SCHOOL PREDATORS*, Amos Kamil's article in the June 10, 2012 edition of the *New York Times Magazine*.

For most readers, this mix of personal memoir (Kamil attended Horace Mann in the 1980s) and investigative journalism must have been a somewhat unsettling way to start their Sundays, perhaps too unsettling to be consumed easily with bacon and eggs or bagels and lox. It was an ugly story of sexual abuse of teenage boys by male teachers, and as such it presented a depressing if provocative scenario of serial predation at an elite private school. There was doubtless some *schadenfreude*-laced satisfaction gleaned from this portrait of pedophiles preying on the children of privilege at a school that most readers could not afford to send their children to.

Yet the article was long, even by the standards of the *New York Times Magazine*—nine multi-columned pages with only a few ads to break up the flow. (My favorite: *"Your son will succeed at St. Thomas More School."*). I doubt that most of the Sunday imbibers of All the News that was Fit to Print made it through to the end. I mean, three dead pedophiles from thirty years ago at the same school? And that's not counting the inference of a fourth pedophile, the former headmaster, Inslee Clark. That's a big pitcher of a very dark brew, too much probably for most readers to swallow on this second Sunday in June, with the sun shining outside, the birds trilling happily and the hammock swaying lazily in the breeze.

But for those of us who went to the school—and especially those who were there during the years in question—it was a revelation, a shock, a bolt of lightning out of a clear blue sky. The amount of turmoil it stirred up cannot be over-stated, as evidenced by the 170 pages of comments that readers felt compelled to contribute. There seemed to be no end to the outrage, agitation and personal anguish that readers expressed. So much so that the *New York Times* finally decided to shut down the option for readers to comment at all.

Some alumnae realized how important it was for this venting process to continue, and they quickly created a Facebook website for this purpose—aptly named "Processing Horace Mann." The only qualification to gain entry was to have attended the school. Once this was verified, it was on to the website and to conversation threads that spun out for very long stretches, seeming to take on a knotty, angst-ridden life of their own. It reminded me of that scene from one of the 1980s *Ghostbuster* movies, where the decompressed ghosts are released from their imprisoning chamber. That's what Amos Kamil had done—apply some gizmo to the collective memory of so many people—including many who'd had no inkling of anything having been amiss during their time at the school—and now the ghosts filled the air, hooting in triumph.

That image was already in my mind on that October 13, 2012, when I walked into the Poet's House, a pleasant if no-frills ground floor meeting room with glass walls that provided a view of the Hudson River and the people strolling on the promenade, where I had just been.

Certainly my own ghosts from the past had been stirred up by Amos Kamil's article, as well as by the subsequent conversations and email postings from other HM abuse survivors. Dreams about Mr Berman and Mr Cullen haunted my nights, while fragments of recollections from that time forty years ago clouded my days. Most disconcerting for me was how some of the darker recesses of memory still refused to give up their secrets. That is, certain events—like Berman's tongue clogging my throat in that motel room—were horrifyingly vivid. But other things, especially the ones that happened in his apartment during my senior year, were still murky, shrouded in menacing darkness, and that disturbed me no end.

But no, the other thing about this event at Poet's House, the main thing in fact, was that this was the first time I would be meeting any of my fellow "survivors," after several months of communicating with them online and by phone. All of them were younger than me, most quite a bit younger—a depressing fact, truth be told. This was one trail I had no interest in blazing, this was one role I took no pleasure or pride in having originated. (Later on, someone from the class before mine would be added to the group, as would another former student from my class—both victims of the music teacher, Mr Somary; but at this time I was at least two grades older than anyone else.)

I couldn't help thinking that if I'd only been more persuasive with Dr Lewerth, if only my complaint had been believed, then maybe I could have changed the course of this twisted history. That may not have been a very rational thought—I had been a moody and insecure teenager, not a super-hero, not a crusading truth-teller—but still, the thought was always there. After all, I am the eldest of four boys, I had always taken seriously the role of older brother, protecting my siblings from harm. But here I had failed even to protect myself, and so many others had suffered.

The first fellow I met at Poet's House, appropriately enough, was Joseph Cumming, the heart, soul and driving force of "Not Alone," the name he had chosen for our group of sex-abuse survivors. Joseph had been mo-lested by Johannes Somary, and the group had started when another victim of Somary's, Ed Bowen, had created a website called "Johannes Somary, pedophile." Joseph had stumbled upon this online and connected with Ed. Both men were informants for Amos Kamil's article, though both insisted on using pseudonyms. Yet here Joseph was, presenting himself in public to the Horace Mann alumnae community for the first time. And soon Ed showed up too, as did the other members of this dubiously-distinguished panel. (Criteria for inclusion: having been violated in some manner by a trusted Horace Mann teacher.)

It was strangely wonderful meeting everyone, putting faces and per-sonalities together with the voices I'd been hearing for so many months now, with the cyber-confessions of outrage, pain and self-loathing I'd been absorbing and responding to at 3:45 AM. (I was one of the few people not based on the East coast, so my very late nights were their very early mornings.) My fellow survivors were only in their early-mid 50s, but they mostly looked older, heavier, weighed down by sadness and personal his-tory. I was glad to be in their company, to offer what I could in the way of friendship and emotional support.

I had become the ad hoc media coordinator of the group, working with an enthusiastic HM alum-volunteer named Alan Ampolsk (a genuine media expert) to help arrange our strategy for dealing with print and TV news people who wanted to follow up on the sex abuse story. Marc Fisher, an editor for the *Washington Post* (and another HM alum), was writing a lengthy investigative piece about Mr Berman for the *New Yorker*. We were in contact with TV producers at *Dateline, Rock Center with Brian Williams* and *60 Minutes* when attorney Gloria Allred came on the scene. Gloria had replaced another lawyer who many of us had become unhappy with. She represented twenty-five of the thirty-six survivors (including me). Her first act was to declare a media embargo, insisting that the threat of nega-tive publicity was a more effective weapon in the negotiations for damages with Horace Mann than more articles and TV news stories could ever be.

She opposed our going forward with this panel at Poet's House (which was taking place on the afternoon of Horace Mann's Homecoming events on their Bronx campus), but many of us didn't agree, feeling it was crucial to explain our position to the HM alumnae community—or at least to as many alums who would make the effort to venture downtown to hear us. There were around thirty hearty souls when we started, but more people kept filing in until all the seats were taken and the meeting room was full.

(Two notable absences were the two brothers of mine whose kids were still students at the school. Neither had said anything encouraging about what I was doing, in fact they made it quite clear that they wished I had not spoken up. My mom was more ambivalent. She had been Deputy Mayor of New York City under David Dinkins, and this was not the kind of publicity she wanted anything to do with. But I had told her the full story of my experiences with Mr Berman a few days after the *New York Times Magazine* article had come out, and she was horrified that these things had gone on without her being aware. "These statements of yours are going to live forever online. I hope you're okay with that" is the most she would express whenever a news story was published.)

The agenda called for all six of us on the panel to give a capsule summary of what had brought us to this point, then the moderator—Rob Boynton, an HM alum and Professor of Journalism at NYU—would ask us questions relevant to our situation, followed by a discussion with the audience.

I was the first up, and I stumbled through my presentation, dwelling on my repeated (and unsuccessful) attempts to alert the school to what was going on. I was the only one on the panel whose experience was with Mr Berman, so I stressed what a dangerously twisted person he was, given complete freedom by Horace Mann administrators to molest at will. (There were two other victims of Berman in our group, both a few years younger than me, both professional men with families who didn't want their identities disclosed; and then there was Jon Seiger, who had been molested by Headmaster Inslee Clark and several other HM teachers, Mr Berman among them.)

The other panelists described in fragmentary bursts the agonies they were put through by their abusers—Somary, Tek Lin, Mark Wright, Stanley Kops and others. Joseph Cumming said there were between twelve and twenty-one predators operating on the Horace Mann campus between 1967 and 1997—he claimed to have heard credible testimony about at least eighteen. Many alumnae remarked that there had to be some kind of collusion between pedophiles; some kind of cabal, how else could abuse on this level have gone on for so long? Another alumnus read a statement by a woman who had attended HM. She had been raped by the English teacher that the school had hired to replace Mr Berman, after that new English teacher had gotten her high in his basement. Then (according to her statement) this male teacher had continued to stalk and terrorize her, following her to college, where she had rebuffed him. The teacher-rapist had then called the young woman's parents, weeping, protesting how much he loved her.

A woman physician who went to HM spoke about how the survivors needed validation from the school, how we had gone through something terrible and life-altering that had made us feel marginalized. "The experience of being molested in itself makes the victim feel worthless," she said. "There is an almost unbearable cruelty in the way the school has continued to demonize them." She lamented that as a result we would never be healed, never be given what we needed to find peace of mind and move on with our lives. "They just continue turning their backs, after all these people have suffered."

In fact, two months to the day after *High School Predators* appeared in print, the Horace Mann Board had issued their response. "We as trustees are saddened and appalled by reports of abuse by past faculty members," they wrote, adding that "Doing the right thing about the past has vastly different meanings to different members of our community." They followed up this bit of double-talk with four more pages of bobbing and weaving. Their bottom line was that "our primary fiduciary responsibilities and legal obligations are to the school today and to its 1,800 current students." The letter was so carefully-worded as to be meaningless. It reminded me of the fine print on car leases. ("Hey, sorry you had a bad ride, but the window to make a complaint has closed shut, so have a nice day and don't let the door hit you on the way out.") In fact, I would have preferred something more straightforward to this Texas two-step, which made such a pretense of hand-wringing, while simply using our pain as an excuse to reassure the parents of current students that everything was fine and dandy at the school now.

And what did we, the survivors, want, besides an apology and a payout for all that the school had failed to protect us from?

We wanted an Independent Investigation into the scandal, one that the school not only condoned but also cooperated with—something that they have repeatedly and steadfastly refused to provide.

We wanted to know how such predatory behavior could go on for so long at such a high profile institution as Horace Mann.

We wanted to know how come there was no mention of such a

widespread problem during that entire period, much less any discussion within the community about what had been taking place?

We wanted to know why no teacher at Horace Mann had ever been publicly disciplined, even when a few had been (covertly) forced to resign?

We wanted to know why Horace Mann had covered up so many incidents of abuse over the years—and what were they still covering up?

We wanted to know why they were so afraid of an Independent Investigation.

We wanted to know why they weren't as determined to get to the bottom of what had happened as we were.

We wanted to know how this could ever have happened.

We wanted some answers, some justice, some truth.

But it didn't look like any of these was going to be forthcoming any time soon.

One alumnus reported that he had just come from Homecoming Day at the Horace Mann campus, and the school was thriving. It was showing no ill effects from the *New York Times* story, having apparently landed back on firm ground, happy to keep the Bad News Bears (we survivors) at a distance. "A thriving Horace Mann is not going to be in any frame of mind to change its ways or to do anything except to keep burying the past," the alumnus told us.

I saw his point.

Meanwhile the sun was setting, and the ghosts flew around Poet's House, circling crazily.

Part Two

CHAPTER 1

Alas! what boots it with uncessant care
To tend the homely, slighted shepherd's trade,
And strictly meditate the thankless Muse?
Were it not better done, as others use,
To sport with Amaryllis in the shade,
Or with the tangles of Naera's hair?
— from *Lycidas* by John Milton

NO ONE TOLD ME THAT THERE WERE no vegetables in France. That is, I'm sure there *were* some vegetables in France, but back in the summer of 1970 I couldn't seem to find any in restaurants, and—being a serious vegetarian at the time—I also couldn't find much else to eat while I was there. There was bread and cheese, of course, not to mention all the red wine I could drink (if only I could!—I got drunk so quickly back then), but at some point I just lost control of my meal schedule and pretty much stopped eating with any regularity for the rest of the summer. So I went over to Europe weighing around 155 pounds and came back thirty pounds lighter. At 5'10", with my long tangled brown hair, I looked a bit like the Scarecrow from *The Wizard of Oz.*

For some reason my parents didn't completely freak out when they saw me. Or, if they did, they just didn't say so to me.

There were only two weeks left in the summer, and I spent them up in Nantucket with my family, four growing boys and two adults crammed into a small rental cottage. I couldn't sleep—I had pretty much stopped sleeping during my last month in Europe—and I recall hearing my parents whispering intimately in bed at around 3:00 AM. Somehow that was alarming, and it made me feel even lonelier and more hopeless.

(My mom was aware enough of my unsettled state and of my dread at returning to Horace Mann to offer to help me transfer to another high school for my senior year. But I couldn't do it. I couldn't make that kind of mental adjustment to a new environment and to new classmates—if such a switch could even be made on the verge of one's senior year. In any case, I didn't feel like I could do it, which I guess was more to the point.)

When I did fall asleep, I had terrible nightmares. Some were too awful to think about, others I wrote down. Here's one:

I am lying in my bed in my family's apartment, and in the bathroom directly in front of me—the door to which is wide open—this desirable girl is in the bathtub taking a bubble bath with two guys, both a good deal older than me. She is fondling the one closest to me, and he is in exquisite pain, almost as if the passion she's stirring up is torturing him. His expression is animalistic, almost too excruciating for me to look at. I seem to remember being flooded with a sort of envy as I watched this take place.

Most of the nightmares were peopled by Mr Berman and Mr Cullen and others from Horace Mann. One dream that I recorded was actually kind of pleasant. In it, I returned to school after this summer and went immediately to see Mr Cullen. He was there with a roomful of other students, but suddenly it seemed as if I'd been away for many years and was returning like the prodigal son. "Oh my God!" Mr Cullen exclaimed, completely shocked at seeing me, as if he'd thought I was dead. *"Suddenly such a wealth of love welled up within me that it crushed the breath out of me, and I fainted,"* so the dream itself blacked out. But then I came to, and the dream resumed with me being placed in a chair very delicately by Mr Cullen. *"We talked so well that soon an hour had passed without either of us being aware of it in the slightest."*

But more typical was this dream of August 21st, which was "suffused by the spirit of Mr Berman":

It seems that I returned to school for the fall semester and chose three courses, among them soccer, because I had to complete a Phys. Ed. requirement. The soccer coach was Mr Warren [another English teacher at HM, who was also my outward bound instructor]. *I found to my surprise that I enjoyed playing soccer, especially when our team won its first game. I remember being at practice with my brother Richie* [two classes behind me at HM] *and an athlete-friend of his. Then Mr Warren gave our squad a big rousing speech, which concluded with his telling me, "You should drop your courses with Mr Berman. It's too dangerous." This drove me into a fury, I started screaming at Mr Warren that he had no right to talk about such things in a public forum, these were private matters that should be kept private. Mr Warren was in a frenzy too, he urged me vehemently to drop Berman from my life, saying that Berman was "a madman," even if he did know German and French. Mr Warren was so worked up that he began speaking in*

Japanese. I finished the argument—apparently winning it—in a flourish of in-dignity by exclaiming, "Life must be like great music, passionately triumphant!" This seemed to demoralize Mr Warren. I was congratulated by a person next to me, who I think was my classmate Arnold K. [who I believe was in fact on the soccer team]. *I confided to Arnold, "Now all I want to do is cry."*

I had stopped communicating with—much less playing with—my younger brothers, and I'm sure they were confused about what was going on. I spent most of the day time on my bicycle, pedaling out to the most remote beaches, where I would sit by myself, gazing out at the Atlantic.

My most vivid memory from that time was whizzing down a hill on my bike and feeling so free. "I could be anyone right now, anyone!" I remember thinking. "If only I could jettison my memory and become someone else. If only I didn't have to be me!" When I got to the bottom of the hill, a small blond boy was standing there, watching me. I slowed down to say hello. "What do you think you're doing?" he asked me. I sped up and moved away as fast I could.

As if to underscore this wish to escape my own reality, I began speaking with a slight but pronounced British accent. This of course brought me a good deal of well-deserved scorn when I returned to Horace Mann for my senior year. I didn't care. My only real friend there now was David Burstein. Tall, curly-haired, gentle-natured and brilliant at everything he undertook, David was the only classmate who showed any interest in what I'd been through; he was eager to hear my thoughts about the paintings I'd seen over the summer and what I'd been reading.

David had been named the editor of *The Manuscript* by Mr Cullen—a blow to me, since I'd been sure I was going to get that position. But David didn't gloat in the least, in fact he was good-hearted and generous, saying how much he looked forward to reading any new work I had. Together we signed up for several classes with Mr Berman, including his Melville class, his John Milton class, and his Russian Literature class (which focused mostly on the novels of Fyodor Dostoievski).

This may sound odd, I know, given all that had gone on between me and Berman, and given the complaint I had lodged. But the truth was, that summer alone in Europe had eroded my resistance to Mr Berman. Losing Mitch as my best friend—that was a blow. Mitch was tough inside, cool, savvy, detached, he didn't buy into anyone else's way of looking at things, including Mr Berman's. His swagger rubbed off on me, giving me something I otherwise sorely lacked. After he had crushed me with his "I wish you were dead," I felt lost, adrift—and vulnerable to someone like

Berman, with all his answers. If only he would have me back.

Yes, it's painful to admit, but that's what it had come down to. Berman had a ready-made universe that I could inhabit, an intricately-constructed philosophic and behavioral system that I could plug my heart and mind into. Isn't that the definition of a cult? Sadly, yes. But that's where I was at that moment. I had lost hold of my sense of self, and I was looking for something—anything!—to fill the void. Mr Berman seemed like my best (maybe my only) chance for salvation.

Accordingly, after the first class of his that I attended, I waited by Berman's desk for my classmates to leave. I asked him how his summer had gone. He said something about having spent a lot of time over at Mr Cullen's. I asked Mr Berman if he had seen any trace there of the letters I'd written to Cullen from Europe—I'd never received any replies. Mr Berman said that, in fact, he had seen my letters unopened, bunched together with a rubber band. Cullen had told him to toss my letters in the trash—a request that Mr Berman had complied with. (Or so he reported.)

Picturing the scene, I died a little inside.

"You look sallow," Mr Berman said.

"I haven't been sleeping well," I confessed.

"You've lost a lot of weight, haven't you?" he asked.

I nodded.

"I want you to come to my apartment this Saturday," he told me. "We've already lost a great deal of time."

He told me his address, and we agreed on a time. Then I left.

Mr Berman lived near Columbia University—on 111th Street between Broadway and Amsterdam Avenue, if memory serves. It was an old pre-War building, a little dingy, with a spacious lobby, long hallways and high ceilings. Waiting for the elevator, I definitely had the sense of doing something forbidden. I hadn't told anyone that I was coming here. (Even though I was tempted to tell David Burstein, it had been difficult not to.) I had a fleeting impulse to leave, just run out of the building and into the street; but it was too late for that. I was here. This was going to happen.

A few moments later, Mr Berman was opening the dark heavy door, and I was in the apartment. He walked me over to the sofa, where he indicated I should sit. I took a quick glimpse around. This was the strangest place I had ever been.

From what I could see, it was one large room, cluttered with things. The place smelled musty, like a second-hand bookshop. There were books all around, bookshelves on the wall, Academic journals stacked in a corner. There was a harpsichord in one part of the room, a dark piano in another.

There was a turntable and a huge collection of Classical records. There were paintings on the wall, some very odd (like a big orange face against a dark background), others familiar—framed reproductions of Renaissance paintings. But the objects that dominated the room, and that still dominate my recollection, are the two large sculptures, over-sized heads, one of Leonardo da Vinci, the other of poet Dante Alighieri. The pieces were of similar size and mass, around 5 ½ feet high with a wide, square base. They were light brown in color (I think), with large facial features, precisely resembling the engravings that were made of each during their lifetimes. That is, the sculptures were iconic, they attempted to convey a sense of largeness and greatness, and there was nothing in their creation that made you wonder about the sculptor. They were monuments to each great man's accomplishments—reverential, even obsequious; the opposite of self-referential.

"You made these?" I asked Mr Berman.

He nodded.

He asked about my summer, what was troubling me, not letting me sleep.

"It's death," I said. "I just see it everywhere. What's the point of doing anything? We're just going to die."

"True enough," he said. "But why worry? What good will that do?"

I shrugged. "I don't know, I can't help it. I see death everywhere."

"It will come when it will come. Ripeness is all," he said, quoting *King Lear.*

(Death was Berman's big subject, just like sex was Mr Cullen's. They were the two taboo subjects of that time, never talked about in my parent's house, never mentioned on TV, never discussed in middle-class circles. It may sound like I was just sucking up to Mr Berman, telling him what I thought he wanted to hear. Not true. That's what I was genuinely thinking about. And it did give me a sense of relief, talking about it. The only other adult I could ever talk to about this was my maternal aunt, a Professor of Psychology at NYU.)

There was also one other living being in the room, a gray male Siamese cat with transfixing yellow eyes. He leapt up off the floor onto a table, glaring at me. Mr Berman told me his name, but I don't remember it now. Berman went over and stroked the gray Siamese, who preened possessively under Berman's touch. I've heard from others who visited Berman that the cat screamed at them. I don't remember that happening. I also don't recall sneezing, even though I'm highly allergic to cats.

Berman stopped stroking the cat and sat down next to me on the sofa.

He took off his thick, black-framed glasses, blinking at me. "I'm losing my eyesight," he told me.

"Really?" I said.

This was terrible news. But now his wearing sunglasses inside made sense—of course! So it wasn't really that weird.

"It's getting worse all the time," he confessed. "In ten years I'll be totally blind."

"Oh, how awful!" I said, feeling very uncomfortable. (What else could I say?)

"I'll need someone to lead me around, like the boy in *Oedipus at Colonus*," he said, putting out his hand. "Will you be that person?"

"Sure, yeah, okay," I told him. "I mean, I hope it doesn't happen, but if it does. . . ."

Berman took my right hand and smiled at me—well, not exactly smiled, it was more like an expression of gladness, though there was sadness in it too—but definitely no humor. I tried to smile back.

"Why did you lose so much weight?" he asked, changing the subject but still holding my hand.

"I'm a vegetarian, but I couldn't find anything to eat in Europe."

"That's not healthy," he told me. "That has to end."

"What?"

Berman stood up, still holding my hand, and he guided me into the kitchen, a gray, separate room. I felt like a little kid visiting his strange uncle. He pointed to a chair next to a small breakfast table (Formica laminate, I think), and I sat, watching Berman make a roast beef sandwich on white bread with lettuce and mayonnaise. He cut it in half on a diagonal, then he set it down in front of me and told me to eat.

"I don't eat meat," I said.

"I respect your moral values," he said, "but you're endangering your health. It's important that you take better care of yourself. Come on, you know that I'm right."

I took a deep breath and sighed. I'd been a vegetarian for almost two years, something that coincided with my interest in Zen Buddhism. I had even worked on and off in the kitchen of a health food restaurant in the East Village called The Cauldron, along with a hippie friend of mine. But I was taken off-guard by Mr Berman's attentiveness, his concern for my well-being. It really seemed like he cared, and I didn't want to lose that, I didn't want to disappoint him. So I picked up a sandwich half—which was difficult for me to do, even painful—and I took a bite.

I saw Berman nod his head and sort of smile in a self-satisfied way.

"Could I have something to drink?" I asked.

Berman opened the refrigerator and poured me a glass of orange juice. I drank some and took another bite of the sandwich. Berman looked almost happy, in a paternal sort of way.

I remember that, as I ate, Berman made some comment about how raw and nervous he was when he started teaching at Horace Mann, so much so that he used to outline his lesson plan the night before every class and then go over it again in the morning—"but now I don't give it a second thought, I just talk about whatever comes into my mind," he said. .

Somehow the conversation got around to Berman's *List of the 1,000 Greatest People Who Ever Lived.* I think I told him that I had taken it with me to Europe and studied it there. "So where would you be on the list?" I asked, only half-serious. After all, only dead people qualified, and I didn't think Mr Berman would actually give me an answer.

"Funny you should mention that," he said, "because just in the last few days I passed Herman Melville to become number twenty-seven on the list."

I was stunned. "Really? How can you measure something like that?"

"I have my ways," he said.

"How?" I asked.

I was serious now, because I could tell he was too. How could genius be measured? And how could even a genius measure himself and where his talent ranked in the grand scheme? I found the very idea offensive.

By this time I had finished eating the sandwich and drinking the juice. Berman ignored my question, putting the dishes in the sink and turning to me. "I did something nice for you today," he said. "Now I'd like you to do something nice for me."

"Like what?" I asked.

"What can you do for me?" he asked back. "And I don't want a plant."

There was a pause, about as awkward as a pause can be.

I knew what he wanted now, and I also knew that I wasn't going to agree to that. Yet I also knew that if I simply walked away, that might be the end of our association—or the beginning of another hiatus. And I didn't want that to happen either. I had enjoyed our conversations, I had enjoyed his paternal attentions, and I felt like I needed him to keep caring about me.

Berman seemed to pick up on the fact that there were limits to what he could ask for and expect to receive.

"You have a beautiful body as well as a beautiful mind," he told me. "It would mean a lot to me if you would let me see it without clothes."

I flinched, not wanting to do that, wanting to run. But no, I couldn't just run away either. I made a quick mental calculation on whether I could live with doing something like that, with displaying myself that way. I decided I could.

A few moments later, Berman was seated on the sofa. He still had his gray button-down shirt on, with the top button undone. He still had his dark slacks and loafers on, with a small throw rug across his lap.

I was standing a few feet in front of him, amid the cultural artifacts of his large cluttered room. I closed my eyes, pretending that I was in gym class, in front of my locker. I took off my clothes as quickly and casually as I could, as if I was changing for basketball practice, letting the clothes fall at my feet. Suddenly I was naked. The illusion of changing for gym class faded away in the harsh reality of being in a strange apartment with nothing on. It just felt so weird and unreal, like I was in a dream. But I wasn't.

I heard Berman make some gasping comments about how lovely I was, "like Tadzio from *Death in Venice*," or something like that—and then how he wished that he was a painter so he could capture this. It was hard for me to hear with all the explosions going on in my head, all the voices screaming at once. I opened my eyes and saw Berman's throw rug going up and down. I didn't want to see that, so I looked away, catching the eye of his bust of Leonardo da Vinci. Leonardo's eye was cold, distant, judgmental. It just made me feel worse about everything. I looked away.

Berman urged me to touch myself, which I did.

To my dismay, I felt myself get an erection.

Then he instructed me in a firm voice to play with my erection.

I did.

I suddenly wondered where the cat was, the exotic Siamese with the glowing yellow eyes, but to find out would have required me to open my eyes, so I didn't.

The voices in my head were howling like banshees now, I thought that at any moment my head would explode, blood and brain matter would be everywhere.

I masturbated myself to orgasm, letting out a small grunt.

Then I somehow put on my clothes and walked out the door, and I was outside again. I remember that I started running.

CHAPTER 2

Easily was a man made an infidel, but hardly might he
be converted to another faith.
— T.E. Lawrence, *The Seven Pillars of Wisdom*

"VOICES IN MY HEAD"—yeah, sounds like quite the cliché when I write it now. Maybe something out of a 19th Century drama like *La Boheme* or *The Sorrows of Young Werther* (which coincidentally I was reading just then). It conjures up iconic images, like Vincent van Gogh slicing off his earlobe (which I have, maybe not so coincidentally, written a play about). Conversely, it also conjures up movies like *A Beautiful Mind* and other media depictions of full-on insanity.

But I wasn't insane, I wasn't bipolar, I thankfully didn't have a serious mental illness like schizophrenia (paranoid or otherwise), and my voices were very much the product of events that had happened and were happening to me—being molested at eight then repressing those memories, having lots of teen sex that I couldn't emotionally process, getting praised to the skies for the poems I had written when I felt so personally worthless. I thought I could escape my demons by losing myself in books and other intellectual pursuits; but as Oprah and Dr Phil have told the world many times, the demons will always find you. Oh yes, they will.

Of course, I didn't understand any of this then, so these voices in my head scared the hell out of me—as did almost everything else about the turbulent emotions I was experiencing. And it wasn't like I could talk about them to anyone. There were no talk show hosts back then urging us to get help, there weren't psychologists at school or free clinics in every neighborhood the way there are now. I couldn't tell my parents or brothers—the very subject of "voices" was simply too weird to bring up. It was even too weird to talk about with my school friends Mitch, David or Justin, except perhaps as a literary device, a way of conveying a character's inner feelings. But these voices were real to me, all too real, there was nothing "literary" about them, and they threatened to overwhelm me, to throw my personal world into chaos.

Actually, at first these voices *were* literary—wonderfully so. They came to me in the form of inspiration when I was writing my poems, telling me what words to use, what thoughts to express, urging me on. There's a splendid painting by Caravaggio of an Angel whispering into the ear of St. Matthew as he writes his Testament. I always identified with that, first with a glowing sense of communion—yes, that's how it is!—then with a bitter feeling of envy and betrayal—that's how it used to be before life turned against me, before everything went terribly wrong.

Things began going wrong while I was traveling alone in non-English-speaking countries in Europe during that fateful summer when my friendship with Mitch went awry. Without Mitch to hang out with, depend on, there was an imbalance inside me, some emotional lever had been pushed into hyper-drive. The voices began as the normal commands that we give ourselves, like "hurry up, you're going to be late for the train," or "why are you always so clumsy!" except now these seemed to take on a life of their own, independent of me. And the only way I could regain control was by writing. Fragments of poems, of course—fragments were pretty much the best I could do, given how self-conscious I'd become about not being good enough. Such as:

> *No boundaries have I but those self-willed*
> *I soar if Mind has strength to be fulfilled,*
> *The shoulders of a thought*
> *To bear the Wind*
> *Upon the whole world's weight,*
> *And ride the strain—*
> *Propelled like sails by storm*
> *Or men by pain.*

Or:

> *I, crowned with fallen leaves*
> *That harvest winds have swept from fallen trees,*
> *And on my feet the spirit of the wings*
> *On which a young bird glided on the breeze*

And finally:

> *And yet, if Mind has depth in which to fall,*
> *Is not ripe Heaven suffused into All?*

But most of the writing I did was in journals, chronicling the people I came across and the paintings I loved, as well as what I was thinking. For example, after splitting from Mitch when we got to Paris, I met a lovely sixteen-year-old Parisian student named Brigitte and almost immediately fell in love with her.

According to my own belief, I should be thankful, humbly grateful to God, for allowing me even so brief a time with Brigitte, if only for the sustaining hope of seeing her again. But oh, if I just had a little more time to see her, understand her, talk to her in a condition less frenzied than our last night together was, when I could not control my thoughts, no matter how hard I tried. I felt myself gathering strength from the mere sparkle of attention in her eyes every time I spoke. Oh, but for a few moments more with her! Was she even here? How could I lose myself to her in so short a time? All I have remaining is a terrible depression from her being gone.

[Note: I did write the lovely Brigitte a passionate follow-up letter in this vein, to which she rightly replied, "Sweet of you to say, but you don't know me well enough to love me, in fact you have no clue who I am." Very true.]

Of course I wrote reams about the Issenheim Altarpiece of the Flemish painter Matthias Grunewald, after a day of hanging out with it like some kind of Christ-addled groupie:

The Resurrection: The emergence of the Glad Christ (Blake). The guards surrounding Christ's tomb are Absolutely stunned, jolted into a frightening and revealing consciousness, and they are staggering back from the White-Hot figure of Christ, from the blinding power and magnitude of the Sun (Chesterton), rising into a sea of stars. The sheer force of the moment unbalances the very night and topples into spacelessness [sic] every object of the air. Christ is dancing on the wake of his death, shining with Divine Presence. There is most simply (but O, how complex!) a Purity and Beauty in His every movement.

But then again, I also wrote three pages about trying to replace a lost screw from my backpack, the absence of which had rendered the backpack basically useless:

After a few exasperating moments of trying to discover if the right-sized screw was to be found, I eventually had half the department store endeavoring to make sense of my very poor French. It was like a lunatic game of charades, in which scores of strangers were brought together by this attempt to interpret my apparently-unintelligible words. When the saleslady finally (and miraculously!) emerged with the right-fitting screw, the crowd let out a cheer, as if some victory had been won for mankind.

And everything wasn't grim, at least not yet, as I hitchhiked my way across France, often sleeping outside, very close to the road.

I woke up drenched with morning dew, a little after sunrise. I cannot remember ever feeling more refreshed. It is the most blessed coolness that comes from the dew, and it so enhances the rays of the sun when they dry the wetness from one's garments.

My personal favorite from this less-desperate time, though, was something that happened (according to my journal) after a car that had picked me up on the way to Nice was forced to stop at a gas station to deal with a muffler problem.

Another car was also stopped there, with a mother, father, sister and brother inside, already decked out in bathing gear for the Cote D'Azur. The family's daughter was around my age and very attractive, and it was all I could do to keep from staring at her. When I did glance over in her direction, I noticed her studying my features quite intently, and she was not the least daunted by my recognizing this. Soon she took a few steps away from the car, and my eyes followed her hungrily, as she knew they would. She stopped directly in front of me, just a few feet away, and—with one of the most alarming movements I can ever recollect having witnessed—she flipped down her bikini bottom, revealing her pale-white backside. It was a terrible moment for two reasons . . .

[Sorry, I can't transcribe anymore. There are literally two complete pages on why this beautiful girl's mooning me was a terrible thing. Talk about twisted logic. Oh man!]

The decibel level of the voices got much louder after my ugly confrontation with Mitch in Florence. His wish for my death echoed in my head, tinged by his furious rage, along with Mr Berman's contemptuous "You are a fool, Mr Fife." During my last night in Rome, I kept hearing them over and over. It was all I could do to keep from throwing myself into a causeway, where a speeding Ferrari would finally put an end to all the sardonic chattering that kept exploding inside me like a series of depth charges.

The voices quieted almost completely during my weeks in Nantucket, but they returned with a vengeance when I showed up at Horace Mann for the start of my senior year. It became difficult at times for me to concentrate in class, often difficult for me to hear what the teacher was saying over the din of competing imprecations and commands. It was one of the main things that drove me toward Berman. If I lived in his world, maybe the voices would go away, maybe he could help me re-establish control.

And, oddly enough, he did.

I mean, you would think that after my strip routine in his apartment the voices would be louder and more insane than ever. But they weren't. In fact, they seem to have taken off for parts unknown, I wasn't even aware anymore of their presence.

A few days after my visit to *Chez Berman*, I wrote in my Melville notebook during one of Berman's lectures:

I have done something very strange, I think. I have yielded up my identity.

Chapter 3

Mr Berman is, in part, a reassurance for me that what I have
discovered is true, and also for my way of life; I often despise our
relationship, however; he assumes the position of questioner, which
I absolutely hate. There is no interchange; I often see him when
I am at my lowest point, for it is then that I am terrified beyond
thought and need him. I am like Mary Shelley after Percy died,
when she wrote that she is preparing to meet him in the next world;
just like I am purging myself to be able (in a way) to converse with
Mr Berman in his own language. There has definitely been an
upheaval in myself, a reversal of my thoughts and an earthquake in
my spirit, where much that was underneath, hidden, has come to
the surface. But I become flustered with all his questions, they are so
persistently demanding and at the same time distracting from what
I want our interchange to be. He emphasizes my own insignificance
and failure, and this is unbearably torturous, and sometimes, for
me, I think, almost masochistic.

— from my HM senior year notebooks, early October 1970.

IN HIS LONG AND COMPREHENSIVE article about Mr Berman in the April 1st
edition of the *New Yorker,* journalist (and HM alum) Marc Fisher de-
scribes Horace Mann at that time as "a benevolent cult" (is there such a
thing? And "benevolent" according to whom?), and he also writes that
"one group of boys stood apart; they insisted on wearing jackets and ties
and shades, and they stuck to themselves, reciting poetry and often sneering at the rest of us. A few of them shaved their heads. We called them
Bermanites, after their intellectual and sartorial model . . . a small, thin,
unsmiling man who papered over the windows of his classroom door so
that no one could peek through."

   This last detail I remember to be accurate, as is the physical description of
Mr Berman. But at least in my time at the school (I'm five years older than
Fisher), there was no "group of Bermanites" hanging out together like pre-
Goths, sneaking cigs and sneering *en masse* at the poetically-handicapped.

In fact, there was no one else in my grade who was admitted to Berman's inner circle (at least not during my tenure there), and there's only one upper-classman I ever saw at the school who I can even connect to Fisher's description.

That was Adam Pearlman, two years my senior and the brother of a classmate of mine. He was a really clever, witty and good-looking guy who I only knew (for the most part) as my classmate's older brother. But he was always friendly and engaging (and thus very different from most upper-classmen), and I envied his olive skin and movie-star good looks. I recall that he suddenly and inexplicably cut off his bouncy brown locks and lost a good deal of weight, becoming sallow and sullen. He no longer smiled and waved when we passed in the hall. I heard whispers that he was a protégé of Mr Berman, without really knowing what that meant. Was that even true? I don't know, but a few years after graduating, the handsome and gifted Adam took his own life.

The *New Yorker* piece—which to my mind got some things wrong, while also containing many brilliant anecdotes and insights—depicted my friend Arnold K. as "a Bermanite of the first order." But Arnold never cut his shoulder-length hair, Arnold had an active social life with some lovely girlfriends, and Arnold certainly made no attempt to emulate Berman's manner or appearance. Arnold was in most of my classes with Berman, and he was the one person whose notes I would copy when I missed one of those classes, just as I gave him my notes to copy after he'd been absent. But the only interactions I saw between Arnold and Berman were contentious—brief, nasty exchanges right after class or as Berman walked to the faculty lunchroom. As far as I could tell, Arnold loathed Berman, even while admiring his intellectual scope and prowess.

As for me, I certainly didn't shave my head, wear suits of any kind or take up smoking. I did modify my appearance from the jeans-and-tee-shirt look of the previous two years, wearing button-down shirts and blazers, and cutting my hair much shorter. I no longer hung out at the Fillmore East, as I had before, catching John Mayall and the Blues-Breakers, the Who, the Butterfield Blues Band, Country Joe and the Fish, the James Cotton Blues Band and so many more—even Joni Mitchell in one of her first NYC appearances, when she was booed off the stage by '60s stoners waiting impatiently for the hard-edged blues-rock group that she was opening for. No more forays to Madison Square Garden, where I had rocked out to The Rolling Stones, The Band, Janis Joplin and—most outstanding of all—Jimi Hendrix. No more reefer or hash, which I was very sad to give up, but it was not on the Berman agenda. No, Berman was all about sharpening the mind, honing it, expanding it—but not the Timothy Leary way, thank you very much. Knowledge was the goal, acquisition of knowledge, and this could not be retained if the mind was distorted in any way or under the influence of anything but boundless ambition.

I still wrote the occasional poem, like this one, which I gave to my friend David at *The Manuscript*:

THE HOUND

I saw a sand-flecked hound
Breathless to test the tide
Burst through the bobbing grass,
While all the beach around
Stretched silent, stark and still—
No bird could be espied,
Nor sails the breeze could fill.
There was no call for glee,
Just time he had to pass;
Nor end one could have found
For his capriciousness,
Unless it was the sea.
But be that as it will,
In elemental bliss
The hound plunged in the sea:
He did it for the thrill.

And this one, which I didn't show anyone including Berman—in fact, it's been buried in the shallow grave of my unread notebooks until now.

THE BRANCH, THE FLOWER

The branch that bears the brilliant flower
Shall be bare upon the hour.
All that lives and loves shall die.
The branch, the flower—yes, and I.
The stars burn as our monuments.
And so it has been ever since.

Why didn't I show this to anyone, I wonder now? I mean, it holds up okay, at least for me, and it doesn't seem like anything to be ashamed of. But I *was* ashamed of it, of that much I'm sure, deeply ashamed, because it did not seem good enough, big enough, momentous enough. Nothing did anymore. If only I'd had someone in my life then to say "hey, dude, chill out, how can you hear the words over the noise of all that self-torture?" But no, I probably wouldn't have listened, sadly I probably couldn't have heard *their* words for the same reason. As I wrote in my journal at the time, *"I am a bug, an insect; and besides that, I learn, a bug with 'savage tendencies. What then am I to think of myself or hope for my future?"* (And this was pre-Kafka for me; no coy *Metamorphosis* allusion here, just straight out, Berman-influenced self-loathing.)

Looking back on this now, forty years later, I can't blame Mr Berman completely for my dark state of mind. After all, I was living in the room next to where I'd been abused just a few years before, even if I wasn't consciously aware of this. I was the oldest of four brothers in a highly competitive Jewish household, attending a highly competitive high school of mostly-Jewish young men. And all of the sex-and-pot-fueled exploits that had taken place in this room haunted me now like the ghosts of pleasures past, pleasures that I hadn't been able to integrate into my life, my personality, my sense of self—which was at a low-point just then.

My relationship with my family was bad and getting worse. Just a few years before, I spent loads of time with my brothers, playing garbage-pail hoops, pretending to be Walt "Clyde" Frazier or Bill Bradley, flipping baseball cards, swapping sports cards of any kind—very typical All-American boy stuff. I had stopped taking part in these pursuits at fourteen, and I hardly have any teenage memories of my two middle brothers after that except for their eating enormous amounts of red meat at dinner (which undoubtedly influenced my decision to become a vegetarian). My youngest brother Andrew always had a sensitive temperament, though not the inclination to express anything with it. My father reacted to me with a hurt defensiveness—if I wasn't going to pay any attention to him, then he would do the same to me. Sometimes he made sarcastic comments about my reading at the table during meals, but mostly he just ignored me. My mom veered between my father's defensive attitude and more active attempts to break through my detachment.

"What do you think you know? What?" she asked angrily one school night at 3:00 AM, storming into my room and standing over me. "What gives you the right to act so superior?"

"I never said I was superior," I replied, looking up wearily from Schopenhauer's *World As Will*.

"You don't have to *say* it," she fumed. "It's there in everything you do, how you feel like you can just tune us out. So what is it that you think you know?"

"I don't know anything," I said flatly.

"That's right, you don't. You're a teenager," she snapped. "You're seventeen-years-old. You've just started living your life. So don't act like there's some secret you know that the rest of us don't. There isn't."

"You're right, mom, there's no secret," I agreed, wanting only for her to leave. She understood this, and it just made her angrier.

"You can have as many teachers and friends as you want, but you only have one family, and we love you," she told me. Her tirade went on for a while longer, but I had stopped listening. After all, what could I really say?

Now that I am the parent of a teenager myself, I understand the dynamics of this scene better. My mom was desperate and well-intentioned, she said what she said for my own good, or what she felt with a certainty was going to be my own good—something, again, that she felt she understood better than I did. Also, I had taken away her parental authority, and she was determined to re-establish this (once again, for my own good). But what chance did this strategy really have of succeeding? What options was she really giving me?

Best-case scenario, I see through the frustration she's venting to the pain underneath, the pain and the love, and I start sobbing from a sense of all the pain I've caused my family, acknowledging that indeed she knows who I am and what I need better than I do, thus reasserting her parental rights. Yet the chances of that actually happening were not good. I already felt misunderstood, in a fairly-typical teenage way. There was already bad blood between us regarding my assertion of authority over my own life. That is, there had already been a clash of wills (with deference to Schopenhauer), and what was the likelihood that I was going to give power back to dear old Mom over my life?

Just a few months before, I had scrawled in my copy of Sigmund Freud's *Leonardo da Vinci, A Psychosexual Study*: "I am desperately in need of fatherly love and support."

Well, that was Berman's cue to assert *his* authority.

All in all, then, these were perfect conditions for an opportunistic predator like Berman to exploit. As another former follower of Berman's was quoted as saying in Fisher's article, "In a school that made everyone think he was special, this was the hardest guy to have approve of you. I needed someone to talk to, and he offered himself as a counselor."

My mom had a sense of this, and she called Horace Mann to complain that Mr Berman was asserting too much authority over his students' lives and was "displaying cult-like behavior." As Fisher mentioned in the *New Yorker,* the school told my mom in so many words to mind her own business, and then they hung up.

Chapter 4

Why do I sleep so violently?

— from my Horace Mann notebooks, 1970.

WHILE I MAY NOT HAVE SHAVED my head or started wearing dark suits, I still considered Mr Berman to be my mentor, the fulfillment of my wish for a caring father. I chose not to think about how he had violated me with his unwanted kiss. I chose to view my humiliating live sex act in his apartment as a kind of initiation ceremony, a necessary demonstration of my allegiance. Of course I wish now that it was otherwise, and that common sense had given me a different perspective. But I also understand that I didn't feel like I had any choices back then. The loneliness and sense of alienation was crushing me. I had to find a reason for hope, and (oddly enough) that's what Berman had given me. (Of course he had also engineered my isolation, but I didn't see that back then.)

He no longer had weighty conversations with me after class. He no longer filled me with visions of being "the next Dickens." Instead he told me that my education had many holes in it that needed filling if I was going to be a world-class poet. I needed to learn Greek and Latin, so I could read Homer and Virgil in the original languages, "as they were meant to be read." But first things first—I needed to be able to play classical piano. And I was in luck because a former student of his was an excellent teacher. Berman had made arrangements for me to start taking lessons right away.

"But I don't have a piano at home," I told him.

"That's all right," he said. "You will take your lessons at my apartment."

I tried to object that I already had a full slate of classes—this merely elicited a withering look of contempt—and then that I simply had no musical talent.

"You're a smart boy, you'll figure it out," he said, and that was it. He made it clear that the conversation was over.

"Genius makes its own rules," Berman frequently claimed (as Fisher quoted in his article), and this meant, in Berman-world, that if you were a genius in one thing then you were expected to excel in everything. I had my doubts about this even then, as I had plenty of classmates who were exceptional mathematicians but couldn't put together a decent sentence, much less a readable paragraph. I also knew that I had flopped as a guitarist, despite taking two years of lessons from a friendly, knowledgeable and patient instructor. (I mean, I couldn't even master *Blowing in the Wind*, which most moderately-talented six-year-olds could play.) Nevertheless I decided to give it my best shot. Who knew, maybe I did have hidden talents, and maybe this "excellent" teacher would be able to find them.

The teacher's name was Edward Leiter, and he had been Berman's student at Horace Mann sometime in the mid-1960s. He was working at that time at Goldberg's Marine Supplies in midtown on the East Side, and I went over there one weekday after school to get my first assignment—which turned out to be a concerto by Rameau. That is, Jean-Philippe Rameau, 1683-1764, "one of the most important French composers and music theorists of the Baroque era." (Thanks Wikipedia, who represents everything Mr Berman would have hated about an open and democratic access to information!)

When I met with Leiter the first time—not at Berman's, he had occasional access to another piano, though I can't recall where—he played the concerto for me. It was lovely though highly structured, and, well, Baroque. I had about as much chance of learning how to play that as I did of suddenly being able to start reading *The Odyssey* in Greek. I expressed this to my new teacher, who told me to try my best.

"Mr Berman has confidence that you'll be a quick learner," Leiter said.

Really? Well, that made one of us.

As I recall, Ed Leiter seemed a nice enough person, thin, medium height, with straight dark brown hair that fell over his forehead. But there was something off about him, something not quite there. He had a studious manner, but he didn't seem very smart. He had none of that Horace Mann drive and ambition, at least none I could discern. To be honest, he seemed kind of schlumpy, though not particularly friendly. He was in his early twenties, but he seemed more like someone in his early forties—kind of staid and methodical, always wearing that Berman uniform of white shirt, dark tie, dark blazer. He was very loyal to Berman, he clearly revered him, even worshipped him. I won't say he was outright hostile to me, but it became quickly apparent that he wouldn't mind seeing me fail. That is, he gave me some notes, some instruction, but he knew as well as I did that these lessons were pointless, I was going to fall flat on my face.

After a few weeks of this gruesome pretense, I had a lesson with Leiter at Mr Berman's apartment. It was a very strange experience. When I arrived at Berman's, three other people were there (in addition to Mr Berman and the gray Siamese cat). One was Ed Leiter. Another was a shadowy figure I may not have been introduced to—in any case, time has rendered his identity fuzzy for me, and I should probably not hazard a guess as to who he may have been.

Not at all fuzzy, though—that third person in the room, Robert Simon, HM class of '69. He looked like a big little kid, bursting the buttons of his white shirt and dark blazer, towering over the much slighter Berman, but he sounded *exactly* like him. I mean, exactly. At first I thought he was doing a mocking imitation right next to him—how rude!—but then, no, I got it, it came back to me—"the clone"! This was "the clone"! Oh my God. That had been Simon's nickname at HM, and even though I had never met him, that famous nickname had filtered down even to me. He had Berman's gestures, facial expressions, vocal intonations—everything!— except he was twice Berman's size. Side by side, they looked like a comedy routine—the intellectual's answer to Laurel and Hardy perhaps. Or the ventriloquist and his dummy, except in this case it was the dummy who had his hand up the ventriloquist's . . . well, you get the picture.

I wanted to laugh, but of course I didn't laugh back then. Not even a little. And it wasn't a good idea to laugh anyway. Mr Berman would not have approved.

But my piano lesson—now *that* was funny! Eddie Leiter kept showing me how to hold my hands so I'd get better key coverage, and I kept messing it up. Badly. So he'd hold up his right hand and demonstrate again.

"Oh! The Grunewald Christ!" I blurted out, holding my hand up, claw-like.

"What?" Leiter asked, bewildered.

"You know, the white-hot Christ—from the Grunewald altarpiece—in Colmar?"

Leiter nodded, he kind of got it, but he wasn't amused. In fact, I saw a look of pure hatred pass over his face like a very dark cloud that wanted to rain destruction on me. If he could have stabbed me and gotten away with it, I think at that moment he would have.

The fact was, there was a weird feeling in the room—I had noticed it the moment I walked in. There was a tension and an expectation in the air, as if there was some other agenda, some event that everyone had gathered here for, and which we were working up to. But what? Or was it just the tension that came from all of us competing for "Daddy" Berman's attention? (Shades of my home life—I had just exchanged one sibling rivalry for another! Even I, dense as I could be, had an awareness of this at the time.)

My piano lesson was of course terrible, I was embarrassingly bad, and I could just imagine Rameau turning over in his grave. ("*Sacre bleu*, what was I thinking? I could have been a stonemason, but no! I had to go Baroque!") But no one was really paying any attention to me. Berman was conversing with his plus-size doppelganger (Simon) the entire time, and that shadowy third guy was reading one of Berman's books off in a far corner. Eventually the piano lesson had run its course and the tension in the room reached a certain pitch, and it couldn't be ignored. That's when Berman clapped his hands and told The Three Witches—sorry (couldn't resist), the three others in the room to leave. I sensed a certain disappointment. (Why? What were they expecting to happen? Or were they just unhappy that Daddy had preferred my company to theirs?) Then Simon and Leiter and the third guy left the apartment, and Berman pointed at the sofa.

I sat.

"I don't know about this concerto," I said. "It's a little complicated for me."

"Edward is a wonderful teacher. You'll see," he told me.

"I know, but maybe I should start with something easier," I suggested.

Berman changed the subject, he started talking about auction items that were coming up for sale—original manuscripts that were being auctioned at Sotheby's. Something of Mark Twain's, I think, maybe something by Melville too. Berman knew everything about it, which items were going on the block—literary manuscripts, Old Master prints, letters by famous people in history, you name it. "You should tell your parents about it," he said. "It's an excellent investment."

Sure, like that was going to happen—my dad taking investment advice from me! Ha!

I thanked Berman for the information, but I told him that $5,000 (the price of the Melville manuscript) was way more than my dad would ever consider spending.

Berman made some disparaging comment about the *nouveau riche* and their misplaced priorities, then he took off his dark blazer (he wasn't wearing a tie) and sat down next to me on the sofa.

I felt uncomfortable, but I tried not to show it. "He cares about me!" I told myself. "He is getting me free piano lessons, he has a vision of the great man that I could grow up to be! So try to be nice."

Then Berman put his arm around my shoulder and kissed me on the lips.

"Don't," I said, turning away.

"What's wrong now?" Berman asked impatiently.

"I don't want that," I told him. "I mean, I want to want that, I really do, but I just . . ."

"I'm tired of your willfulness," he said. "I'm tired of your acting like a willful and ungrateful child."

"I'm not a child," I protested.

"Then stop acting like one," he told me sternly. He started caressing my hair and smiling at me. Or I think he smiled—I really couldn't look. I had retreated to someplace inside me, where none of this was happening, but I still heard him take off his glasses and place them on a nearby table. I smelled his musky after-shave lotion again as he put his hand on my knee, nuzzling my cheek with his nose.

No! I couldn't take anymore.

I got up and said, "I have to go," then walked toward his apartment's front door.

Berman's mouth clenched tightly, but he didn't say anything, though I could feel his eyes following me, and the intensity of his rage was terrifying.

I let myself out.

Chapter 5

I love another, and yet I hate myself.
— Petrarch

I have often tried to obliterate my self with hatred, rather than lose it in love.
— from my Horace Mann notebooks 1971

I DIDN'T GROW UP IN A RELIGIOUS HOUSEHOLD—far from it. While my brothers and I all had our turn as Bar Mitzvah boys, Judaism was really just a social custom for us, a form without substance, something you did because you were supposed to, and it would somehow be wrong if you didn't. But to feel any *need* for religion, or for what religion might have to offer—that was considered bizarre behavior, just as wrong—no, probably more so—as ignoring religion completely. But during my summer alone in Europe, that's exactly what happened.

"I feel a huge need for religious succor," I wrote in my journal, *"for a feeling of enlightenment that can only be provided by a religious zeal, an ardor of the soul aspiring toward the source of all Divine Love in the universe."*

And elsewhere in that summer's journals: *"The human soul without a God is whirled around in the abyss, in the lonely existence that surrounds it where there is no faith."*

My dreams were filled with religious imagery as well as with literal angels and demons; as in this description I wrote after awakening in the middle of the night.

"I was sitting in a room, and there was some activity in it which I cannot recall; then suddenly I was seized by what I recognized as an Angel of God—at that moment I had the realization that this is what Dante and Milton must have felt. The Angel wore a simple blue piece of clothing, like a shepherd might. The Angel spun me around, I remember feeling violent passions and emotions that almost killed me, they were so strong. Then I remember being directed to 'write something great,' and I saw in a vision (in the dream) what I was supposed to write about. But then this vision vanished, as did the Angel, and I was left alone and wanted to tell someone about it, but there was no one to tell. And now I can't remember what it was I saw in the vision. What really galls me is that I felt in the dream

that this was the great Vision I'd been waiting for, that I'd been put on earth to write about, and now I can't remember what it was."

There was even one time in Florence that summer—and I hesitate to reveal this, because it seems so unbelievable and, well, *muy loco*—when I had my very own mystical vision. Yes, strange but true. I was alone in a darkening chapel at sundown—I believe it was in the church of Santa Maria Novello—where there was a statue of Christ by the brilliant Florentine sculptor and architect Filippo Brunelleschi, barely discernible in the shadows. Suddenly the sculpture was struck by a beam of light, *bathed* in bright yellow light, as if from the setting sun—but this was impossible as I had already seen the sun descend past the window high in the arches. I looked around for someone else who might be seeing this, but the guard and the few other tourists were in another part of the church. Then the burning light—because that was the impression this light produced, as if the sculpture itself was on fire—went out in a moment, as if a switch had been flipped. I ran out of the church into the street, wanting to tell someone what I'd just witnessed—but who? And what could I really say? Even at seventeen, I was not unaware that this was a good way to get oneself locked away. So I told no one, I didn't even write much about it. I felt queasy even thinking about it. I still feel so right now.

Of course, all this mystical activity must have had a great deal to do with my being under-fed, sleep-deprived and alone in a foreign country where I didn't speak the language. And then there were all the Christian paintings I was looking at in most of my waking hours—Christ on the cross, Christ driving out the moneylenders, Christ at the Last Supper. (I saw loads of Baby Jesuses and thirty-three-year-old Christs, but where was the teenage Jesus? Why didn't he get any love, any attention? I never saw a single depiction of teen Christ—of Jesus at *his* Bar Mitzvah—which probably goes back to what I wrote before about the awkward years of young Jewish men. You can't exactly build a serious religion around a pimple-faced kid, now can you?)

My over-heated religious phantasms were probably fueled as well by the fact that I was re-reading the Bible just then while also reading Dante's *Divine Comedy* (in English translation). Strange ways for a young Jewish guy from the big city to spend his summer vacation, no doubt, and it produced these very strange results.

But after my big reveal in Mr Berman's apartment, these religious yearnings morphed into something else entirely. Berman was my God now. I put all my faith in him.

"Anything that Mr Berman says, by virtue of his saying it, is the truth," I wrote in my school notebook that fall. *"Even if he makes a statement and five minutes later states the exact opposite, then they are both necessarily true. This is so even if he unthinkingly said the second when he meant to reiterate the first. There exists the assumption that whatever appears to us contradictory only shows our incomplete perception of the truth."*

But what was it exactly that Berman believed?

There were two mighty cornerstones of *Bermanism*, now my new religion, and they went hand in hand—which, of course made them even easier to build a belief system on. One was that humanity could be divided into "geniuses" (.00001 of the population) and "mediocrities" (everyone else). The other was that the only people who mattered or should be cared about were "the great men"—which included those very few women of genius, the only ones to crack the top 500 of Berman's List: Wanda Landowska (musician), Emily Dickinson, Virginia Woolf, Elizabeth I (of England), Sappho and Jane Austen.

Here are some entries from my notebooks at that time:

"A mediocrity knows nothing else except mediocrities."

"In the graveyard in Parma, Italy, there are 400,000 people buried, all of whom have been given up to oblivion except one—Niccolo Paginini [the famous violinist and composer]. *That is the proportion of the pervasive mediocrity of the world to genius."*

"All great men with true and honest insights have proclaimed the insignificance of the material world, and that it is a burden to the soul."

"The duty of a great man to the world is to convince all men of the existence of a Heaven that is beyond their grasp now, though ultimately attainable; and he serves as an example of that greater something after which it is possible and necessary to strive."

"Great men, the greatest men, that is, have never restricted themselves to that in which they believed. Their endeavors were by nature so profound and large that they over-swelled any set belief that they could safely be said to have represented."

This last entry relates interestingly (or at least it seems so to me) to a paragraph I wrote down directly from something Mr Berman had told me after one of my visits to his apartment, and which states with great succinctness Berman's view of human history.

"[Understanding] *the Patterns of the Universe: we are in the maze and so cannot behold its intricacies except so far as our individual intelligence yields us a perspective. T.E. Lawrence* [that is, Lawrence of Arabia] *on War* [in his magnum opus, *The Seven Pillars of Wisdom*], *Leonardo* [da Vinci] *drinks from the source. Only the gods* [are above the maze and] *can see from on top, but even they are the stuff of which mazes are made. Leonardo knew perhaps, but it is doubtful that he could have articulated it* [due to the restrictions of human language]. *But even if he could have—and if ever a mortal man was capable of doing so, then Leonardo was—there would have been none who would have understood. But even if there were some who could have understood, then these people would not have been able to act upon that understanding. But even if they* [hypothetically] *would have been able to act on this, then their actions would have to be inconsistent with those Patterns of the Universe, which were impossible to comprehend."*

Shortly after Mr Berman had told me this, I had a dream which seemed to elaborate on Berman's worldview.

"I just dreamt that Mr Berman tells me that all that philosophically matters is that we realize that all things exist in 'sets,' and that nothing extends over the definable boundaries of its particular 'set,' which set is defined by these limitations. No object in that set can possess any characteristic other than that which can be made generally applicable to that set, and which could be called an attribute of all the objects in the set, to a greater or lesser degree. Thus nothing is individual, but is merely important as regards its relation to the other objects in its set. The relation of the 'sets' to each other he said nothing about."

In going back over my students notebooks and papers—most of which I have somehow been able to preserve through many moves, a disastrously-failed marriage, another failed long-term live-together relationship, and several vehement requests by my mom to toss the box containing my papers into the garbage—I came across one of my earliest poems, an untitled (and unfinished) poem/novel that I started when I was fifteen and continued working on at sixteen. It's about a family who lives an isolated and rather tortured existence in a castle. (And no, I hadn't read Kafka's *The Castle* yet, I don't think I'd even heard of it.) It begins:

CHAPTER I

Will I ever rise to hail the dawn,
Rising with the birds, their songs;
Always just beyond my grasp.
Will my doubts ever be stilled,
My age is too small
To fall victim to merciless despair,
Always a loner in search

Of a path I alone will walk . . .
My father screams at me.
He laughs and cries and says I am hopeless.
"A scarecrow cursed with a straw mouth. . . ."
I wander thru villages within myself.
Frightening faces amid a still young land. . . .
am I strange
am I strange
I perceive only the timeless beating
Of furious waves against a fragile shore.
I bury myself under the sand,
Beneath the ripples that are me.
Why must it be that I am able to convey
My thoughts only to those who will
Understand my silence?

I worked on this poem long before I even knew about Berman, yet some of the imagery seems to presage him and his worldview in ways I can only describe as "strange" (to use my favorite word of that time) and somewhat chilling. [Note: I have edited this in some very minor ways for purposes of length and clarity.] Such as:

CHAPTER III

Amazed.
I am amazed
For I perceive
An ancient maze.
My astonished gaze
Perceives an ancient maze
Where once there was a castle;
Enclosing me
Within an endless night:
I stare long
Down the blind-black columns,
Rows—but I see no end in sight.
I walk so slow
Then swiftly along
An inner path I go:
This path

Becomes a country road—
Straight and narrow it begins
And ends in a twisted grin.
I peer thru the infinite ways
Mapped upon
The brick-baked ground
By drunken footsteps
As if in a daze.
Steps lead to somewhere,
Steps lead to nowhere—
Walking slow
Within a maze. . . .
I am lost among the turns,
Startled by foreign sounds;
I am walking dizzy
Within a maze of madness. . .
The maze becomes
A rolling ship
Rocked by windstorm waves. . . .
I plunge overboard,
And I am washed upon
My homeland shore.
I lay upon the sand
And think no more
Of that madness maze—
For I could not find
Myself still walking
Any of its many ways.

One of Mr Berman's favorite dictums was that there are no accidents.

When I read this poem from my extreme youth, it does make me wonder if I ever had a chance. Was my experience with him, as destructive and harrowing as it turned out to be, simply "inevitable" (to use one of Berman's favorite words)? That is, did I make a conscious choice, or was it all simply destined to happen?

Chapter 6

—Ho, ho, we are in hell! Alone like two wanderers destined for
eternal misery! Ha, ha! We are each other's single consolation on
the lonely road we walk. Ah yes, this is certainly hell. We are but
two misguided, windswept seeds jostled about to yield this crop of
darkness.

— from my 1971 HM notebooks.

AGAINST ALL REASON, I continued my music lessons with Ed Leiter,
working on that Rameau concerto. I did not get any better, and I
may in fact have gotten worse. I am highly competitive by nature, and I
do not like the sensation of going down in flames. But I was terrible here,
simply awful, and all I wanted was for Mr Berman to allow me to admit
defeat with some sense of humor and grace. But he wouldn't do that.

Every few weeks I would have another piano lesson at Berman's apart-
ment. Usually Robert Simon would be there when I arrived, and he and
Berman would converse during my lesson. But the tension I felt in the
room wasn't there anymore, that sense of nervous anticipation was gone.
After the lesson was over, and I had made a complete fool of myself,
Simon and Leiter would exit the apartment, leaving me alone with Mr
Berman.

And each time this happened, Berman would sit down next to me on the
sofa or just across from me and look into my eyes or put his hand out—
and I would flinch away. He would frown and do everything in his power
to break down my resistance to having a physical relationship with him,
pummeling me with lines such as:

"Do you have any idea what an opportunity you are being given here?"

"You're just a middle-class mediocrity like your parents."

"This was part of the mentoring process for the Greeks. Socrates made
love to Plato and Plato made love to his students. It was part of the teacher-
student relationship, the natural order of things, and everyone knew and
accepted that."

"Writers need to be adventurers, if you want to be a writer, you need to try different things, you need to experiment. Don't close yourself off to anything."

But none of these worked on me. None of these changed my mind, even though I wanted to respond differently—not because he was attractive to me in any way, but how often do we have the chance to sleep with our gods? Still, I couldn't force myself to do it, no way, no how, not even as an "experiment"—and I felt terribly guilty. I don't know how else to account for my incoherence when I tried to write about it—this is a selection from a four page rant in my Melville notebook that makes no earthly sense (even to me) but does convey all the anxiety and confusion and self-loathing that the subject evidently filled me with at the time.

My aversion to committing myself to Mr Berman, in which act I would be inherently incorporating all my mortal misgivings as well as my immortal longings, and the result so far has been a frantic desperation. . . . But I wonder how much philosophy is a result of this avoidance and how much is based upon and influenced by these exasperating sexual deviations which can find no peace in this person. I have immortal strivings but this humanity is acutely inhibiting, and I don't know how to conquer it. . . . I cannot extend myself unconstrainedly [sic] to Mr Berman because of this inhibiting factor in me. This is just impossible and intolerable, but it is a woman's embrace that I need, though at the same time [I'm] ashamed of these desires because they are opposed to the selflessness that is my intent and objective. . . . Yet this is torturing to me, as I really do love Mr Berman, but feel that I am not free to assert my desires here. The last thing I crave is normality. . . . I thought that I was striving toward an enhancing union with my greater Self, God, and so to lose my own overburdening self in Him . . . Ah! What foolishness is mortality, all these human diseases, how did I ever fall prey to them? Mr Berman tells me I am going to die, and that once I realize this, everything will follow. But I [already] know this. But I cannot fully feel it until I am free of these accentuating distortions of my perceptions, and also I have no wish to be diverted into the unproductive sterility of normality. Even the vehemence that I display in my earnest endeavors to be disemburdened [sic] even this is implacable falsity that I mistake for passion . . .

Say what?

And that's not the end—it goes on further, making even less sense. This rant—which I have no memory of having written—resembles nothing so much as the ramblings of a coke-fueled Lit Crit grad student on a 4:00 AM bender or maybe a brainwashing session in some prison for the pretentiously insane.

I can't honestly tell if Mr Berman is trying to brainwash me or if I'm trying to brainwash myself into doing something I don't want to (or if there is really a difference between the two). But I have no doubt that the issue at the heart of all this high-flown babbling is: why can't I overcome my own "inhibiting factors" and just give my "God" what he wants—my youthful butt on a platter. But I couldn't, and there was nothing I could do to overcome my revulsion (both physical and emotional) at the very thought of it, much less the reality of his intimate touch.

Whenever I even tried to imagine his having sex with me, my mind just shut down and wouldn't allow me to go any further. Berman was in my dreams, of course, he was one of the major characters, hovering nightly over my prostrate form with his shaved head, fishbelly-white face and coke-bottle-thick glasses, licking his lips at my nakedness. But even there I fought him off, even there I would never allow him to dominate me sexually. And no matter how many times I guiltily wrote about how much I "loved" him, how he was the only person I felt any real affection for, the only person I really cared about and who cared about me—when I was there in his apartment, with him trying to grope me, trying to make out with me like I was some virgin in the sweaty back room at a high school dance—well, sorry but he couldn't get to first base with me. Could not get his hands on the jewels. And the harder he tried, the more "vehemently" (to use a word from my rant) I slapped him down.

Finally one afternoon he exploded.

"You're just as bourgeois as your family!" he screamed. "You're a willful and ungrateful little pipsqueak, and I won't have it!"

"I'm sorry," I whimpered. "I can't help it. I guess it's just not something I want."

"You don't know what you want," he said accusingly.

"Well, I want to want it," I pleaded. "I really do. I just can't . . . "

Of course the logical question to ask right now is: why did I keep coming back? Why didn't I just break off this arrangement between us, which wasn't really working on any level for either of us? That is, he wasn't getting what he wanted (my heart, soul and sexual access), and I was having to endure classical piano lessons (which I hated) and this repeated and unwanted groping. Yet I couldn't leave. Why?

While I'd love to give all sorts of smart-sounding rationalizations that somehow make my now eighteen-year-old self look less pathetic, the reason is right there in my notebooks from that time, clear as can be.

[I have] *the fear that at bottom I am but revenging myself on the world and burning my heart out with superfluous rage; that my quarrel with the world is the result of being personally affronted* [that is, rejected] *and being motivated by petty feelings.*

And also:

Mr Berman is a reassurance for me that what I have discovered is true.

All of which is just a high-flown way of saying that I felt like a fraud—a sad, lonely, friendless outcast—without Berman there to tell me that I was "a genius," that my isolation was the price of being so gifted, so special. But I could feel a tsunami wave of despair welling up just at the edges of my heart, I could hear the whispering voices of madness at the corners of my consciousness. If I walked away from him now, then I felt like these would overwhelm me, drown me in sorrow, demolish me with a terrible roar. With no one else to turn to for support—not parents, not other teachers, no friends or therapists or authority figures I could trust—I was terrified of losing the one person who stood between me and oblivion. But I also couldn't submit to his desires without losing what remained of my self, without giving up the ghost of my own self-worth and independence.

So I felt like I was in hell. Absolute hell. I couldn't move one way, I couldn't move the other way, and I couldn't stay where I was.

So what could I do?

Chapter 7

The intellect is like armor, it guards us from mistakes, but it cannot warm us, cannot give us the life it protects.

— R.H. Blythe

THIS WAS OF COURSE MY SENIOR year at Horace Mann, a school whose entire reputation and *raison d'etre* was based on getting its students into the best colleges. And no matter how caught up I might have been in my own hellish dilemma, I certainly couldn't avoid being part of this process. Horace Mann might not care that I was thin as a scarecrow, that I mumbled to myself in Spanish class, that I had gone from the most popular guy in my class to some sleepless zombie with no friends at all, but they were sure as hell going to make certain that I didn't make them look bad by failing to go Ivy League.

Accordingly I went to see Mr Gucker, the college placement advisor, in his small on-campus office. Mr Gucker was a balding man with bright eyes, a brisk manner and a strong sense of purpose. I believe I had already taken my SAT tests—though honestly, most of that school year is a blur for me, outside of my meetings with Berman.

"I'm worried about you, Mr Fife," Mr Gucker told me.

What specifically worried him was how poorly I had positioned myself for my college applications. Even though I had an A-/B+ grade average, this only qualified me for number forty-one in my class of one hundred two students. (Yes, we had class rankings then.) My SAT scores were around 1410 out of a possible 1600—"a fine total," but nothing special at Horace Mann, where eight students in my class had achieved a perfect score. He recommended that I consider taking the tests again. I said no, I wouldn't. (I didn't have any preparation for the tests, and it was all I could do to keep from walking out of the room when I took them. I couldn't see what they had to do with the process of learning.)

Mr Gucker also pointed out that I didn't have much to recommend me in terms of extra-curricular activities. Yes, there was *The Manuscript*, and all the poems I'd had published. But why had I quit the Swim Team? That would have been very helpful, presenting me as a more balanced student and a team player.

"I just didn't want to do it anymore," I said tersely.

In general, it seemed that the only thing I had going for me was my high scores in Honors English, and the very strong recommendations that Mr Cullen and Mr Berman had written for me. "That's something at least," Mr Gucker said, sighing. But he told me that Harvard and Yale and even Princeton were probably out of my reach. "Don't have your heart set on the Ivy League," he advised. "Take a look at some of the better small schools like Wesleyan and Vassar. Be ready to keep your options open."

My mother was worried too about my college prospects. She was especially concerned about the lack of enthusiasm I exhibited for getting into any particular school.

"College was one of the best times of my life," my mom said (she went to Bryn Mawr). "I want it to be one of your best times too. But that's not going to happen unless you apply yourself and put some work into it. Colleges are not simply going to accept you because you go to Horace Mann. You have to show them that you have a real interest."

She was right, of course, but the problem was that I really didn't have any enthusiasm for going anywhere because I felt so stuck in my present circumstances. I forced myself to look at college pamphlets and applications, and my eyes glazed over, a sentiment that probably hasn't changed much for many high school seniors over the years. But still, it was something that I had to do.

Wasn't it?

Not according to Berman.

"Don't go to college at all," he told me. "Just spend your days at the library, then come back and discuss what you've been reading with me."

"Really?" I asked.

"Do it for a year or two, then see where you are. You can always apply to colleges then."

"I don't know," I said. "My parents would never go for that. They've put a lot of money into my education."

"Oh, so this is about money?" Berman said cuttingly. "I thought this was about your development as a writer."

"But what would I even tell them that I was doing?"

"Just say that you want a year off to think things over. They'll understand."

But they didn't.

"You what?" my dad said, visibly shocked, when I proposed this.

"So you're not going to college now? What are you doing instead?" my mom asked anxiously, as I had predicted she would.

"I'm going to work on my writing," I said.

"Can't you do that in college?" my dad asked.

"Are you prepared to go into the army?" my mom put in. "Because if you're not in college, then we can't protect you."

Yes, there was still a draft lottery at this time, and if your number was low enough and you weren't in college, then you belonged to Uncle Sam.

"I hope you're okay with fighting in the jungles of Vietnam, because that's probably where you'll end up," my mom said.

"He's not going to Vietnam," my dad told her. "I'm sure he'll re-think this idea and realize that going to college makes the most sense."

And he was right.

I had met with soldiers who were about to be shipped out to Vietnam—two years before, as part of my involvement with the anti-war group—and I had seen that fearful look in their eyes, I had heard their pleas that we help them find some way to keep from having to fight a war that they didn't believe in. Even in my current confused state, I was still aware enough of my circumstances to know that I never wanted to find myself in that position.

And I was actually relieved—the scenario that Berman had proposed did seem kind of empty and repetitious, even to a hardcore scholar (as I considered myself to be then). I mean, every day in the library, just me and the stacks? Then spending my evenings fending off Berman's advances? Yikes. I may not have been yearning for kegger parties, but some kind of social life would be nice.

(And what would I have done for spring break? Go visit Melville's house in Pittsfield, Massachusetts? Oh yeah, and then I could have gone to the local Carvel's and purchased a Fudgie the Whale cake and eaten it on Melville's lawn! Woo-hoo!)

I had gotten this idea in my head during my junior year at Horace Mann of going to college at Oxford in England because of its great literary heritage. I loved the Romantic poets, and I just associated that tradition more with England than with the US. And I was fortunate that my mom had a college friend who was married to an Oxford Don, so I was able to get the inside word on my chances of being accepted to Oxford. According to this Don, my chances were zero—at least if my hope was to go directly from an American high school to matriculating at Oxford. Their high school was different from the American one, this professor explained, and I would be required to do two years at an American college in order to be eligible for entry into Oxford. In the meantime, he suggested I take a summer course there, to see if it would be worth all the effort required to apply.

Accordingly, I had enrolled in an eight week course at Oxford for the upcoming summer titled "Shakespeare and his Age," which I was looking forward to. But now I had to come up with a roster of colleges to apply to. I came up with five, including Harvard. Even though Mr Gucker did not think that I stood a chance of being accepted there, my dad had a connection—Martin Petetz, editor-in-chief of the *New Republic* and a Harvard professor—who knew me a bit, had read some of my poetry, and who vowed that he would do everything in his power to overcome my low class-ranking and my less-than-perfect SAT scores and get me accepted.

There was a bigger problem, though, than my less-than-impressive high school credentials. It was my attitude, which—not to put too fine a point on it—sucked. There were several reasons for this, of course, primarily the pressure that Mr Berman was putting on me. He was unhappy that I had caved "so easily" in rejecting his offer to "home-school" me for the following year. He let me know in no uncertain terms that if I did go to college, his choice for me was Columbia University, where he could continue to monitor my progress. He opposed my even applying to any other colleges, but I did anyway. However, his disfavor tainted the entire process for me, casting a very large shadow over any hopeful expectations I might have, just as he had over my future.

I don't have any copies of the essays I had penned for my college applications, or even any memory of them, except for one school that requested a list of the books I had read "for personal enjoyment" over the past year and then didn't believe me when I submitted my list of sixty or so books. However, I do have a copy of a letter I wrote around that time to a man who wrote a "save the sperm whale" article for the *New York Times*. The letter was written at the urging of Mr Berman, and the tone and language and phrasing are all straight from the Berman lexicon, just as all my essays undoubtedly were.

> *Dear Mr Garrett,*
>
> *It just so happens that I was first apprised of the sperm whale's dangerous proximity to extinction on the very day on which your article appeared. I am, however, not surprised, for between the sharkish men and the mannish sharks, what chance has even the great whale, though it be the consummate*

incarnation of power and grace? Its decimation seems to me an even greater tragedy than our own. To take up Melville's metaphor, it only proves how very unpoetical our nation is . . . [I am skipping a number of sentences— trust me, they are tedious beyond belief.] *Your profound indignation was wonderful. I shall write to whomever might be likely to listen. It does not, however, seem to be a subject calculated to arouse similar indignation in the public breast, nor to prove any more popular than the book that sounds its Leviation depths. . . .*

Yikes.

If you're thinking that this sounds more like a letter from a British stuffed shirt in his sixties than an eighteen-year-old NYC high school student who had just recently started to shave on a regular basis, then you're on the right track. Now just imagine you're a college official analyzing application essays, and you receive something written like that. No, not good.

(Contrast that letter for a moment with this paragraph from an essay I wrote *two years earlier* about the tragic events in Biafra, Africa.

"The Nigerian civil war has already killed many times the number of people that the Vietnam War has. Yet the newspaper coverage of this civil war has been sparse at best, at times almost non-existent. When the war has been covered, flagrant errors have often been committed by major newspapers; and the events have been reported mostly from the Lagos side. The media must bear the blame."

I'm not saying it's perfect, but yeah—that's how Mr Berman had "improved" my writing style.)

But if the essays were bad—and I'm sure they were terrible—they were still a paragon of prescience next to my in-person interviews. It says something, first, that I can only remember three of the five colleges that I applied to—Harvard, Amherst, and Columbia. But the memory of those interviews are burned into my brain with the vividness of, say, being caught pissing in a public fountain.

The Harvard interviewer was a sophisticated silver-haired man wearing a bow-tie. As I recall, he and I spent the interview trying to out-snob each other. He made some nice comments about my poetry, and then he mentioned some poets he liked who my verses reminded him of. I told him that I disliked one of his poets—it might have been James Russell Lowell, who in fact had gone to Harvard. In any case, I know we got into some nasty spat about James Russell Lowell and the Transcendentalist School of Poetry. He was amused by my impudence at first. By the end, he wasn't amused any longer.

I was really excited by the prospect of going to Amherst because of its connection to the poet Robert Frost, whose work I was very taken with at the time—mostly because of Berman, of course. (He was Berman's favorite American poet, the only one who made it into his *"Top 100 Who Ever Lived."*) But I also liked the idea of getting out of the city and being part of a new community. Unfortunately, I screwed this one up from the get-go by mixing up my dates and arriving on the campus a week earlier than my interview had been scheduled. The only school official who was available to meet with me was a crotchety old man with a few white hairs on his big bald head. This man had actually been friends with Robert Frost, close friends if I remember correctly. That should have been something that brought us together, a mutual interest. Instead I argued vehemently with him about which were Frost's strongest poems. It seems I did not win the argument.

But of all my bad interviews, the one at Columbia University was without a doubt the worst. The interviewer there was a graduate student with dark, floppy hair and a very high opinion of himself.

"So I see you were Honors English," he said. "Which writers do you like?"

"I don't *like* writers," I corrected him. "There are writers I love, and there are writers I hate, and there are writers I don't really care about."

"Oh yeah?" he said, sensing a challenge to his authority. "So there are no writers you *like*?"

Well, let's just say that things went downhill from there, very fast, especially when the grad student put his sneaker-shod feet up on the desk that was between us.

"Please don't do that," I snapped. "I don't want to look at the bottom of your dirty shoes."

Well, the guy went ballistic after that, just ballistic! He threw a pencil at my head (he missed) and hissed at me through his teeth, "If it's the last thing I do, I'm going to make sure that you do NOT get into this school!"

So yeah, my chances of spending the year in the library and playing "hands off the salami" with Berman just got a whole lot better.

Chapter 8

I once said to Goethe, as I was lamenting the disillusionments and vanities of life: "After all, an absent friend is no longer himself when he is present."

To which Goethe replied: "Yes, because you yourself are the absent friend, and he is only a creation of your mind; whereas when he is present, he has his own individuality and follows his own laws, which do not always correspond to whatever ideas you happen to have at the moment.

— Arthur Schopenhauer

OF ALL THE HUNDREDS AND HUNDREDS of paintings that I had looked at and loved since Mr Berman had introduced me to Renaissance art, the painting that I loved most was "Paradiso," a canvas by Giovanni di Paolo illustrating the conclusion to Dante's *Divine Comedy*. It was not the best or the greatest or even the most memorable painting I had seen—not by a longshot. But I just loved the image, which simply showed a group of Italian men and women conversing in a wooded field. Yes, there was the story element from Dante's poem, that these were saved souls who had achieved eternal Paradise. And there were Giovanni's subtle harmonies of composition and color that drew the viewer in to a world where nothing was hidden, where nothing could be hidden, because there was nothing to hide anymore—there are no secrets in Paradise. But no, these were not the elements that made the image so important to me, so special, that caused me to gaze at the reproduction I had of it longingly for hour after hour. It was this universal and cosmic sense of understanding and being understood. It was this lovely feeling of peacefulness, of being able to talk with friends without drama. There was no anxiety or competitiveness here, no cruelty or confusion, no uncertainty or despair, no money or achievements. Everything was so simple, so easy, there was no struggle involved. Everyone accepted each other and enjoyed each other's company, everyone was happy to be here, because there was nowhere else to be. Literally. This was Paradise. There was just *here*.

And that's what I wanted my life to be like. That's what I wanted to have in my life. And that's what I didn't have—not even a little.

David Burstein was still the only friend I had, but even with David there were times when we weren't actually friendly, when what linked us instead were things like jealousy, envy and a rivalry for Mr Berman's approval. David was very smart—in fact so smart that he would get into all the colleges that he applied to. And he was a very good Cassio in the school production of *Othello*, while I had lost the ability to act, after having been very comfortable on stage until I hit my teens. But David couldn't really express himself very well, not in creative writing terms anyway, and I clung to that as something I could still do better than him.

We met up on one Saturday evening in February, a little past the middle of our final year at the school. Something was bugging David, he seemed nervous, agitated, more so than I had ever seen him before. As I wrote in my journal later, after coming home: "

It was as if he wanted to tell me something that he himself didn't know, or if he did know, then he thought it would be detrimental to tell me. But detrimental to who or to what?"

David started off by saying that he wished we were better friends, closer friends, the kind of friends who could tell each other things.

"But don't we do that already?" I asked, even though I knew it wasn't true. I hadn't told him anything about Mr Berman. Not about the kiss at the DC hotel, not about going to Berman's apartment, and certainly not about stripping naked and jerking off or fending off Berman's predatory advances. How could I tell him? I couldn't even imagine my mouth forming the words. And yet if there was anyone I could tell, it was David. He would understand, he wouldn't judge me. But still, I couldn't do it.

David launched into a description of a dream he'd had the night before. In the dream, he and I were together in David's bedroom, and his father [a doctor] walked in and asked who I was. According to David, I had a bundle of books under my arm, all by Tolstoy, and I told David's dad, "I am Tolstoy." David's dad received my remark with respect. David felt that if he (David) had said it, then his father would have laughed in his face. David added that he was surprised in the dream that I called myself a disciple of Tolstoy's (though what I actually said was "I am Tolstoy") instead of a disciple of Mr Berman's.

"What made you think of that?" I asked, suppressing some nervousness.

"I don't know, I guess because we're in a lot of classes of Mr Berman's together, and there's always a lot of competition for his praise."

"Right," I said, breathing a sigh of relief.

Then we discussed David's dream a bit more, and he told me that his father was putting a lot of pressure on him to enroll in Pre-Med once he got to college and to become a doctor.

"Are you going to do that?" I asked.

"I don't know. I hope not," David said. "I just feel like that would mean giving up on myself, giving up on any chance for having my own life."

Could this be what was bothering him? It didn't seem likely. David and I had had many conversations before about our distant fathers, and I had never noticed him being this nervous. But if this wasn't causing his agitation, then what could it be?

Chances are good that we probably also spoke about a mysterious girl who had begun auditing Berman's Russian Literature class. Around our age with dark-hair, pale skin and lovely brown eyes, she seemed to come straight out of the pages of a story by Pushkin or Chekhov or Dostoievski and to be the embodiment of what each of us yearned for in our personal *Underground Man* fantasies. But she wasn't a fantasy, she was very real, sitting at a desk in the back of the classroom and taking notes with methodical intensity, never looking around, never favoring any of us with a word or a glance (much less a smile), and then hurrying down the staircase and out of the building as soon as the class was dismissed.

Berman, for his part, never referred to her presence, which just deepened the mystery. Who was she? And how had she gotten permission to do this, to be there, since there were no other girls in any of our classes, and none of us could even remember hearing about a time when there had been?

Oh, I wanted her, I wanted her so badly.

She seemed to have materialized out of nowhere and to be the answer to all of my lonely prayers. It wasn't just that she was beautiful. She was also serious, intelligent, sensitive. This much was evident (or so it seemed to me at the time) from her demeanor.

I pictured her naked, rising from the desk and sidling over to me, kissing me on the lips.

This of course gave me a raging hard-on, something I felt very weird about having in Berman's classroom. (Though it was oh so appropriate to the world of Dostoievski's *Notes From The Underground* and *The Brothers Karamazov*, which we were studying at the time.)

Marc Fisher, in his *New Yorker* article, gives her real name and states, "The boys concocted stories about her identity, calling her "the Dark Lady of the Sonnets."" I don't recall any such designation or group discussions, though it's possible that other "boys" in the class were having them. I spoke about her occasionally with David, mostly to speculate on who she was, where she had come from, and what her connection to Berman was. But the sexual feelings she inspired were too hot and heavy to speak about, at least for David and me. We adopted the detached tone of scientists discussing a particularly interesting lab slide when we brought her up. It was only in the silence and isolation of my bedroom that I could really dwell on her image and the impact she had on me. Did I masturbate to my fantasy of her? Without a doubt. She also strode through my dreams, a slender, high-breasted, but still mysterious figure. This was the only place it seemed where we would ever speak, much less touch, and, even more unlikely, kiss and make love.

But really, who was she? And why was she sitting among us? And why hadn't Berman said anything about her—not even to me?

It was around this time that I went to Berman's apartment again. I think he had suspended the piano lessons, saying that my college applications did not leave me adequate time to prepare. (But I'm not sure about the specifics—to some degree, my meetings with Berman at this apartment blend into each other; that is, the conversations are clear and distinct, but when they were said and the sequence in which they unfolded often aren't.) I wanted to ask Berman about the mystery girl, but I didn't dare—if he wanted to inform me, then he would do so in his own way whenever he chose to. I remember telling him about going to the Metropolitan museum and marveling at paintings I studied there by Sassetta, Simone Martini and Andrea Mantegna. (The latter two are in Berman's top 100, the first one only makes it into the second hundred.)

Berman closed his eyes and sighed. He was stroking his Siamese cat, who sat on his lap. He told me, "I wish that all the great paintings in the world could be put into a capsule and launched into space, far away from the stupidity of human beings."

"But wouldn't that defeat the purpose?" I asked. "I mean, the paintings were made for people to look at. What would be the point if no one could see them?"

"The point is that they would be safe and no harm could come to them. That is more important than whatever some no-neck family from Milwaukee might have to say about them."

I didn't agree with Berman, but I said nothing more on the subject. It wasn't like I was going to convince him of anything.

Berman then began speaking about one of his favorite subjects: Einstein's brain. As an amateur paleontologist, Berman was fascinated by Albert Einstein's brain, which he claimed to have seen. He said it was twice the size of the normal human brain, and that it was "blackened"—that is, it had been thoroughly used. "Most humans only use 10-15% of their brain capacities; Einstein used 85-90% of his. That is the meaning of genius."

(Berman often spoke to me about "the human brain" and "the brain pan" and how most people waste theirs. That was supposed to be one of the main purposes of his "mentoring" me—to get me to use my entire brain, to "blacken" it, just as he (Berman) was doing. He also spoke about how men had greater brain capacity than women, which was why there were so few females on his list of *The 1,000 Greatest People Who Ever Lived.* I didn't particularly believe this, since many of the smartest people I'd ever known were women, including my mom. However, it did make my ego feel better for all the isolation and alienation from the fairer sex that I had experienced since breaking up with Lisa the previous year.)

"Where's your passion? What happened to it?" Berman suddenly asked me.

"What do you mean?" I asked back, hurt, my voice cracking.

"I had such hopes for you, you were so full of life, your writing was so full of passion. But now it seems to have dried up. What happened?"

I shrugged. "I don't think that's true," I said.

"I don't have sex only with men, you know," he said. "I have a thirty-seven-year-old Bulgarian mistress, and when we make love, she leaves marks from her fingernails scratched on my back. I was hoping to bring out that kind of passion in you, hoping that it would bring passion back to your writing, which has become flaccid and dry."

"That's not true," I repeated, tears welling up in my eyes, leaking out, no matter how I tried to suppress them. "You don't know what I'm writing now. I haven't shown you anything for a while."

"I'm sure you would have, if you had something to show. That's how I know that you've lost your passion. When you first came into my class, the poems were just oozing out of you, you couldn't find the time to write all of them down. But now you've become rigid, your river of inspiration has dried up. What can I do to help you find it again? That is my only concern."

"I really like that girl who sits in on your class," I said, almost under my breath.

"What girl?" he asked, clearly not expecting this.

"The dark-haired girl who sits in the back during your Russian Literature class," I reminded him.

"Oh, I see," he said. "And you'd like to have sex with her?"

"Yes," I said in a small voice. I couldn't actually believe that I was saying this out loud, it was the kind of hidden desire that I never expected to speak to him about.

"I could arrange that," he told me.

"Really? You could?" I responded, starting to feel excited just talking about it.

"Certainly. If you really think that would make a difference," he said.

"Oh, I do. It would. I feel sure of it," I told Berman.

Berman nodded, looking directly in my eyes.

"But where would I meet her? I mean, how would this even happen?" I asked.

"You'd meet her here, of course," Berman said.

"So she'd come here to meet with me . . . because you told her to?" I asked again, trying to figure this out.

"Yes. She'll do anything I tell her to," Berman said, adding that he would let me know when the date had been chosen.

Wow. I really hadn't expected this.

Wow.

Chapter 9

The lower a man is in the degree of consciousness, the more natural the sexual relationship will be.

— Soren Kierkegaard.

CHAOS REIGNED.

Pandemonium ruled.

The inmates were running the asylum of my heart and mind.

Yes, I was bouncing off the walls of my bedroom with all the feelings that this assignation with Berman's mystery girl was stirring up in me.

Was it a good idea?

Was it ethical?

Should I talk with her first? If so, what should I say?

Will Berman be in the room watching us?

What should I wear?

In my fantasy, Berman opened the door of his apartment, and the mystery girl floated in, looked me in the eyes, then kissed me on the lips. I put my arms around her, held her tightly in an embrace, kissed her deeply. She reached down, started unzipping my pants, while I unhooked her bra and reached under her skirt . . .

Then everything got kind of fuzzy.

Do I slip on the condom or does she slip it on me?

Should I ask what her name is?

What about the cat, where is he?

And, again, where is Mr Berman?

I didn't like the idea of there being nothing real between us, she might as well be a hooker and Berman her pimp. At the same time, I didn't like the idea of spoiling the mystery either. There had never been a word between us, not a single word, and yet I felt so attracted to this girl, probably more attracted than I had ever felt to any girl. To add words now would just be a desecration, it would mean spoiling something perfect.

After sex, then we would talk. Then there would be time for words. Not before.

With that decided, I felt a little easier in my mind, the pressure seemed to let up a bit. My thoughts turned to Berman's callous remark about my writing—that my passion had dried up, "gone flaccid." Was this really true?

I had been working on a few different poems, but the fact was, I didn't have any perspective on my own work. I couldn't tell if they were any good. But I didn't want to show them to anyone either, least of all Berman. In my current state of mind, even the most minor criticism would send me over the edge. And the truth was, most of my poems were in pieces, and most of the pieces didn't fit together to make any larger whole. I had lines like:

> *He showered us with shiny stars*
> *To distract us from our inner scars*

And:

> *Nothing that has the power to please me can.*
> *All I see around me are figures who shadow forth doom*
> *And fill my nostrils with odors of the inevitable tomb,*
> *I don't even know where or how these feelings first began.*

I did have one poem that seemed to fit together, but it was strange, different from anything else I had written, and I didn't know what to do with it. It was inspired by Mr Berman's admiration for Robert Browning's *My Last Duchess*, which is a dramatic monologue in the form of a poem. (In fact, Berman told me that he had written a monograph about the poem that was going to be published, and he had promised to give me a pre-publication copy.) I decided to try my hand at my own dramatic monologue poem, and—after many failures and terrible drafts, I had written something at 4:00 AM one night/morning that came out all at once, of a piece. But it scared me, it was so weird, and I couldn't even think of a title. Or who the main character was, delivering the monologue. Here it is:

> *We quashed the insurrection,*
> *As you asked.*
> *Now the sacrifices are piling up*
> *On your stone altar,*
> *And the seething legions are restless.*

The useless smoke
From all that burning flesh
Just clogs our nostrils now
And makes us choke.
You are unimpressed
With all your triumphs
And do not respond
When I ask what you want next.
You won't even agree
To look down on me,
Your humble servant,
From your marble throne.
How can you be so unkind,
After all that has been said and done?
What, sir, can I do
To appease your misery
And regain my own peace of mind?

I was excited at first by this poem, so oddly different, and I brought it with me to school to show it to Berman. But then I backed off, wary of how cutting he could be. The fact is, I'm not sure what worried me more, his rejection or his praise. Both involved having to live up to expectations that terrified me.

But then an idea occurred to me—yes! I'd bring this mysterious poem with me to Berman's apartment and show it to her, the mystery girl. I'd ask for her help on it, ask her to give me some notes. Then I'd tell her how much I'd like to see her writing, whatever she was working on. (I was certain she must be a fellow poet, or at least a short story writer.) This would give us something to talk about and make it less awkward after we'd been together in coitus. That is, unless the fantasy happened exactly as I'd imagined. In which case it wouldn't be awkward at all. Right?

But any confidence I had in this plan just fell apart when I went to Russian Literature class a few days later and saw the mystery girl herself seated there, writing diligently in her notebook.

This was insane! Who was I kidding?

This beautiful, intelligent girl, this paragon of young womanhood— she wasn't just going to walk into Berman's apartment and throw herself into my arms and make love with me. That could never happen, not in this lifetime.

Or could it?

She was here, wasn't she, at Horace Mann, in a place where no other young woman had ever been seen, a fair maiden floating blithely on a sea of testosterone?

I tried to catch her eye and get a smile. Nothing. Not even a glance. I took a deep breath and looked directly at her for a full moment. She gave no indication at all that she had even noticed.

Still, it seemed impossible that she would be here in our midst, but there she was in the flesh, blinking, taking down notes. We hadn't simply imagined her, she wasn't our collective fantasy, and she had come to this place to hear Berman. Who's to say that she wouldn't come to his apartment as well? Maybe he had her under some kind of spell, like the evil wizard he often seemed to me to be.

Yes, it's true, amid all my "love" for my mentor, I was also increasingly resentful, even fearful, of him.

How could Mr Berman control my thoughts?" I had written in one of my course books. *"Isn't that the only way I have of retaining some semblance of clear sanity?*

I had also written in one of my journals:

I wonder if Mr Berman always has music playing [on the turntable] when I come [to his place] because he is [really] in the midst of listening? [Does he do it] for me, in expectation of my arrival, and as a sort of inducement to familiarity and intimacy?

The more cracks I saw in Berman's façade, and the more I even entertained the idea that he could be manipulating me for some purpose not to my benefit, then the more my "clear sanity" felt deeply threatened. At times it felt like my world was falling apart again, this little world that was held together by my pledging obedience to Mr Berman in all things except the one thing that he wanted most, but which I wouldn't give him— couldn't give him, for fear of losing that last vestige of what I knew as my self.

It was at moments like these, when I doubted my allegiance to Berman, that the feelings of madness would come on again. There was no one to speak to about them, nowhere to go to seek comfort. I went to my mom a few times and told her that I'd like to look into the idea of seeing a therapist, that I felt like I could use some help. My mom said no, she didn't agree with that and wouldn't allow it.

"In this family, we don't tell our secrets to strangers," she told me. "And besides," she added, "once you start down that road, when will it ever end? It could go on forever." If I wanted to talk something over, why not talk with her?

But how could I do that when my relationship with her and my dad was such a big part of the problem? The fact that I didn't feel like I was being heard or understood at home—well, wasn't her refusal to let me see a therapist just one more example of that?

It got to the point that I even brought up the subject of talk therapy to Berman when I was over at his apartment. I mean, I knew he was a huge admirer of Freud and Carl Jung, so wouldn't he also believe in the practical applications of their work?

"All that is fine for other people, but when it comes to genius, the therapist must put down his pencil." (This was a paraphrase, I think, of something that the novelist Vladimir Nabokov had written. At least I seem to recall Berman saying as much.)

Again, that just went along with Berman's larger credo that "Genius makes its own rules." Genius to him was an excuse for being the exception to every rule that applied to "other people," it was like being designated a prime number that could not be broken down into smaller components, while "everyone else" was just a subset, a variation on that primary theme.

Accordingly I wrote in my notebook, *"I am wondering now upon the accuracy & usefulness of psychiatry and psychoanalysis with genius."* But that didn't make me feel any better, and it didn't make the bad dreams go away. (That is, when I was fortunate enough to sleep at all.) I started reading everything I could by Freud and Jung and their disciples, hoping (I guess) to figure out my own problems and heal myself. I got so involved in this, so immersed in this mindset of neurosis and emotional conflict, that I asked my parents to buy me *The Collected Works of Sigmund Freud* for my eighteenth birthday. They did. I immediately dove into all twenty-four volumes like a leper seeking a cure. And I found a lot to mull over in the cases of "The Rat Man" and "The Wolf Man" and the other wounded freaks that he treated, and of course I found all their symptoms in me.

But I still didn't feel any better. Not any calmer or any happier.

As I wrote in my journal, *"I am plagued again by fantasies of devils, little devils, that infest the region of my body."* I didn't know what magic words I could recite that would make them go away or stop them from stabbing me.

I also lashed out at the world, writing, *"Truly, I believe this world to be abominable."* But it wasn't the world I hated, it was myself, and what I perceived as my own weakness.

I hated to admit how much pain I was in, because logic seemed to dictate that this meant that I wasn't a genius. Genius made its own rules, but I was asking to play by someone else's rules, to achieve a measure of the "normality" that Berman sneered at. He seemed to be saying that this pain and despair was my legacy, a sign of my "significance" and something that I should treasure, be proud of.

But it was too much for me, I couldn't bear it, and I couldn't go on this way. I couldn't even contemplate a future composed of days and nights like the ones I was currently going through. I had to believe there would be some relief in the future.

Maybe with the mystery girl.

Maybe that would provide the key to turning things around.

Maybe, after that, everything would be different.

Chapter 10

If a man realizes the hell that he is enduring, if he really grasps it, why can't he then transform it into heaven?

— from my HM 1971 notebooks.

ONE OF THE MORE FASCINATING ASPECTS of Marc Fisher's article in the *New Yorker* is the quotes he was able to get (or to cull) from Mr Berman and his two remaining disciples, Robert Simon and Edward Leiter.

Leiter, my former piano teacher, responded to the many accusations of abuse against Berman by stating, "I suspect that at some point these souls have stared at themselves and felt the failure and unhappiness of their lives and . . . have constructed a desperately conceived reason . . . that explains and ameliorates the failure, emptiness and misery they see before them."

Berman responded in a similar vein. "I can comprehend that sundry people are (were, will ever be) both insensately vindictive and—not wholly unrelated—unhappy with what they perceive in rare encounters with the mirror as failed lives, and are commensurately eager to compose or pursue tangible causes for that in the form of other people with whom they might have had tangential contact a long while since."

At a Horace Mann Reunion in 2009, Robert Simon told a classmate who had mentioned dark rumors he'd heard about Berman, "I hate to burst your bubble, but I was never sexually involved with Berman, and I'm not even gay." Leiter chimed in that he wasn't attracted to men either. Berman wrote to Fisher, "I had no sexual desire for Mr Fife—or any student for that matter. . . . My interest was, and is, in women."

So yeah, just some regular guys, looking to score some lady love on a Saturday night at the mall.

(Note: just for the record, my issue is not with their sexual preference, it's with their being such bold-faced liars.)

Berman denied every aspect of my account, saying that it was composed of "inventions . . . a manner of desperation born of a self-perceived failed life." He denied that I had ever been to his apartment.

Which I guess makes me some kind of true evil genius, to have some-how been able to record all these descriptions of events and internal con-flicts in my notebooks from 1969-71, just so I could take some kind of demented pleasure (I guess) by publicly flogging my oh-so-innocent high school teacher with them forty-three years later. I mean, the rationale is hard to figure, to say the least. Even if I was "insensately vindictive"—and I submit that only a world-class narcissist/misanthrope would use a word like "insensately" there—then why would I choose a high school teacher to vent my "vindictiveness" on? Especially one who, according to him, I'd had only "tangential contact" with "a long while since?" I don't want any money from him, and God knows, he has no reputation to sully. So what exactly would my motive be?

Frankly, I have better things to do in my present life than to dredge up events from the distant past that are still very painful for me, and that are somewhat embarrassing too. I have a teenage daughter now, and I'm not happy for her (or for anyone else for that matter) to see me depicted like this. I'd much rather deal with this material—if I dealt with it at all—in a fictional format, where I could pick and choose what to reveal and would be allowed the option of hiding behind a character's mask when things got too close for comfort.

But sometimes the unvarnished truth has to be told, especially when it concerns something as serious as child-abuse and teen-abuse, and when it involves an institution like Horace Mann that refuses to own up to its failures, refuses after all these years to set the record straight, open up the files and allow for some emotional healing. Thirty years of ac-tive abuse involving fifteen to twenty abusers (according to the Bronx District Attorney's office), with countless young lives damaged or ru-ined—you'd think the school would go out of its way to cooperate in get-ting to the bottom of how something like this could ever have happened at such an "elite" and "prestigious" place, America's shining high school on the hill. But they have done just the opposite.

Of course, abuse on that scale can't happen without a careless admin-istration that doesn't concern itself with its students' day-to-day welfare. (Unless the head of the school is also one of the abusers—which was the case after my time, but not during my years at the school.)

In the days leading up to my rendezvous with the mystery girl at Berman's apartment, I was a bleary-eyed zombie wandering the grounds of the school, but no one took any notice, frankly no one cared—I was a senior on my way out, my college applications were already submitted, the school had done its job (as far as it was concerned). There had never been any follow-up to my complaint against Berman in the previous year. No one had ever checked with me to make sure that the problem had been taken care of or wasn't going on any longer. No mention of the problem was ever made. Why would they, after having succeeded in silencing me and covering it up the first time?

The liaison at Berman's took place on a Saturday afternoon in March. He didn't give me much advance notice, maybe a day or two. He told me what time to show up, and I did, nervous as hell, my dramatic monologue poem and an old condom stuffed in my pants pocket.

I walked in and sat on the sofa, looking around. The mystery girl wasn't here. Where was she?

"She isn't coming," Berman told me.

"What? But you promised."

"I did what I could," he said. "Frankly, she finds you repulsive. I couldn't overcome her disgust."

I jumped to my feet. "I don't believe you!" I shouted.

"Sit down," he told me.

I slowly sat.

"It's her problem if she can't see your beauty," Berman said. "I see it shining so clearly. I will always see it."

All of a sudden he was on top of me on the sofa, holding my arms down, pressing his lips against mine. I felt disoriented for a moment, surprised, caught off-guard. A part of me felt beaten, defeated, it didn't want to fight anymore. So what if he has sex with me? What's the big deal?

But I've always hated bullies of any kind, and I did not like being physically manhandled; also I was bigger than Berman. Strong as he was—and he was surprisingly lithe and powerful for a sedentary person with such a slight frame—I managed to throw him off and run for the door, not looking back.

I never came back to that apartment.

(Though of course, according to Berman, I had never even been there at all.)

Chapter 11

I wanted to know how the human mind reacted to the sight of its own destruction.

— Carl Jung, from *Memories, Dreams and Reflections*

ONE BY ONE THE RESPONSES CAME BACK from the colleges that I had applied to, and one by one I was rejected. Amherst, Harvard, and the other two colleges (whoever they were) all wanted nothing to do with me. I felt numb and was hardly aware, though my parents were very upset. I had told them how badly the interview went at Columbia, and none of us held out much hope.

What was Plan B?

I had no idea. "B" no longer stood for Berman, that much was for sure. I suppose it stood for "Back to the drawing board" now. But I couldn't take it in, couldn't think about taking any alternative action. I was just limping along from one day to the next, trying to make it through to graduation day. I went to Berman's classes, but I had no contact with him outside of that. The mystery girl probably still showed up to Russian Literature class, but I can't be sure. If she was there, I didn't notice.

I had the home telephone number of Mr Cullen, the other writing guru, and I gave him a call, saying I was in a bad state and needed to speak with him. His voice was flat, devoid of excitement. He told me to come right over.

Mr Cullen lived alone in a spacious apartment on Riverside Drive and 103rd Street. I'm sure he had a wonderful view of the Hudson River, but it was nighttime, and I wasn't in a sightseeing mood. I was desperate, frantic. I felt like I didn't have any self left at all. I was smoking cigarettes—not a good idea under any circumstances, but especially for me, since I had asthma. But my anxiety levels were off the charts, and I didn't know what to do with my hands when I wasn't smoking. It calmed me down enough to make it possible for me to think. Otherwise I just had one panic attack after another. (And no, I wasn't smoking Mr Berman's brand, Benson & Hedges.)

Mr Cullen ushered me into his living room. He seemed sullen, morose, almost disinterested. "What's going on?" he asked.

I told him about everything I'd gone through with Mr Berman. I didn't leave anything out, including the sexual incidents. He did not seem surprised.

"I told you to watch out for him," he insisted.

"You told me that he was the most brilliant person you knew, and the best teacher you'd ever come across."

"Yes, true, but I said that he was all head and no heart, and that he wasn't for everyone."

I shrugged. "I feel like he's taken everything from me, including my love of writing."

"Why didn't you come to me about this before?" Cullen asked.

I told him what Mr Berman had said, about how my letters to Cullen from Europe had been tossed into the garbage unopened.

"That's not true," Cullen said. "I read your letters. I didn't realize you were expecting any formal response. I thought we'd talk about them some time at school, but then you started avoiding me. Now I know why."

I nodded. "It just really hurt me."

"I'm sorry this happened, but you made a decision. I'm sorry it didn't work out."

There was a pause. I stubbed out my cigarette in an ashtray.

"What can I do for you now?" Cullen asked.

I told him that I needed his help in finding a therapist. I explained that my parents didn't want to pay for it, and I didn't have any money.

Mr Cullen shook his head. "Sorry, but there's nothing I can do for you," he said.

I told him that I was having suicidal thoughts, and I was afraid of what might happen if I didn't get some help.

"That's between you and your family," Mr Cullen said. "I have my own problems."

Mr Cullen said that he was in love with someone who wouldn't return his affection. This had thrown him into a deep depression, which he was trying to deal with.

"Can't you just give me the name of someone to call?" I pleaded, awkwardly lighting up another cigarette. (I may have been the world's most awkward smoker.)

Mr Cullen shook his head. "I'm sorry that things have gone so badly for you, but right now it's all I can do to get out of bed in the morning. I just don't have it in me to do anything else."

Mr Cullen ushered me out into the hallway and firmly closed his door.

I felt a sob rise into my throat. I took a final puff of the cigarette and stubbed it out. Here was this man who had predicted such great things for my future. Now I felt like I didn't have a future of any kind.

How had everything gone so terribly wrong?

The days seemed to stretch on, one after the other, with nothing to fill them. That seemed unbearable.

But then something happened, something unexpected. I received a letter of acceptance from Columbia University. (I can only imagine how upset that grad student was, the one who had thrown the pencil at me and then had failed in his quest to get me rejected.)

This was good, this gave me something to look forward to, a place beyond Horace Mann. It helped to quiet the suicidal whispers in my head—something for which I am still deeply thankful.

I don't remember anything about graduation except I somehow forgot to wear a tie (how un-Berman-like of me!), and they wouldn't hand me my diploma unless I was wearing one. I had to improvise a tie by using one of those plastic strips that hold curtains together in a neat bunch. Then they gave me my diploma. It was over. I had made it all the way through, I was finished with Horace Mann.

In my recollection, I went away to Europe that summer—first Oxford for eight weeks, then Alsace-Lorraine and Germany for a month—and made a clean break from the two writing gurus who had dominated my life for the past two years, Berman and Cullen. But my notebooks tell a different story. In one notebook, there are drafts of letters to each of these mentors, describing my travels and the paintings I'd seen, telling each how much I missed him. Pathetic—yes, I know. I never sent the letters, of course, but they're a good indication of how desolately lonely I was, and how the memories of these two twisted men were my most constant companions.

The Oxford course was subtitled "*Shakespeare for Americans*," and that's what it was, all thirty-seven plays of the Bard, along with his sonnets and other poems, plus three or four other plays by fellow Elizabethan or Jacobean playwrights, presented with all the patronizing head-patting that this subtitle suggested. Most of the Americans were high school or college teachers, and there were only three of us under twenty-years-old—me, a nineteen-year-old college student who had just finished his freshman year at Skidmore, and a high school senior from New Jersey whom I will call "C." C. was a smart, shy, beautiful girl with long chestnut-brown hair that blew in the breeze. Of course I fell in love with her right away. We were friendly for a while and hung out together, enjoying each other's company, discussing the plays we had read. But then I became too demanding, and she pushed me away.

The course was taught by an English poet with a very high forehead and an even higher opinion of himself. He interspersed his lectures on the Bard's plays with anecdotes about spending his weekends on a yacht with "Dick" Burton and "Liz" Taylor. I have no idea if these tales were true, but the lady high school teachers in our group couldn't have been more impressed. We had occasional "mixers" where the liquor flowed freely, and I observed our vaunted poet on several occasions, stewed to the gills, with his hand up one or another of their dresses. Somehow he had found time to take shore leave from the violet-eyed Liz to get to know some regular Americans too.

For my part, after the ardor had cooled between me and C., I hung out mostly with a blind woman in her late twenties with straight reddish-blond hair and a raven-haired woman in her mid-twenties whom I nick-named "the sad girl" because, well, she always seemed very sad. Here is an account from my journal:

Tonight I walked with the blind woman and the sad girl, and I made them both laugh with spontaneous stories, and I felt no worm sicken the rose of my sincere good cheer, even though it was contrived solely to gladden them. And it gave me the most acute pleasure to feel their joy, for a moment I could lose my pretensions and my self-consciousness and be but a vehicle for their delight.

Please keep in mind that I was eighteen-years-old at the time, not forty-eight, so I trust it's pretty clear that I hadn't lost any pretensions, and I was still a paragon of self-consciousness. As much as I liked the blind woman and the sad girl and still have fond memories of them, I'm pretty sure that they were simply the only people in our group as lonely and socially-outcast as me. So make no mistake, it was they who were doing me the big favor by hanging out, not the other way around.

But after a while even they couldn't stand my know-it-all attitude and my constant quoting from scholars like Maurice Bowra and G.B. Harrison (who, by the way, was Berman's mentor at the University of Michigan— oh, did I already mention that? And I hope it's not too obnoxious of me to keep bringing it up). After a few weeks of our eating meals together in the burnished-wood diningroom with the portraits of famous Oxfords Dons lining the walls, I would suddenly see the blind woman and the sad girl pick up their trays and dart out into the hallway as soon as I made

an appearance. Of course, there were awkward encounters after the lectures, when we were jostled together by the departing crowd, but that
was pretty much the end of our time together. Every now and then I'd
see the two of them coming out of a shop or walking down a street in
Oxford, arm-in-arm, happily laughing together without the aid of me or
my "spontaneous stories."

Oxford is a beautiful place, one of the most beautiful I've ever been to,
emerald-green glades with the River Thames winding through them; and
the university campus and grounds may be the most stunning and awe-
inspiring of any in the world. It was a pleasure to wake up in the morning
(whenever I'd slept, that is) and walk out into the sunshine and be among
such architectural splendors. But, like most places (and people) that one
puts on a pedestal, Oxford too proved disappointing.

This was the place where I had hoped to matriculate, where I felt like
I could belong, but that wasn't what I experienced—quite apart from my
exile within our group. At this time the dollar was very strong against the
English pound—hard to imagine now, I know—and there was a backlash
against Americans and our purchasing-power that could be felt on every
level, even by an otherwise-oblivious student-type like me. And then some
of the young Englishmen there—blond, pale-skinned students, who really
did "belong"—somehow these blokes picked up on my being Jewish (was
it the kinky hair? The tortoise-shell glasses? Or the know-it-all attitude?).
Often garbed in athletic wear, having just punted the Thames or sprinted
off a cricket court, they hurled hate-laced invectives, lavishing a dose of
anti-Semitism on me that was a new experience (nothing like that in NYC,
to be sure!) and not a welcome one. I soon canceled any plans I might have
still harbored about coming back here on a more permanent basis, and I
resolved to keep to my room for the rest of the course.

This room was on the ground floor of one of the college dormitories—
Christ College, I think, though I can't find any confirmation of this in
my journals—and it was less a room than a stone cell. At first I liked this
ancient-feeling, this lack of American amenities, but then it just started to
feel oppressive, as the stone walls began closing in. I have a very strong
memory of looking in the horizontal mirror over the bare sink and hating
what I saw—the Berman-influenced face of a serious scholar, a pedant. I
looked and felt fifty years old. Where had the young poet gone, the poet I
had gloried in being, the poet who couldn't find enough time in the day to
write down everything he had on his mind?

I resolved to write a completely new poem while I was there—something I had quite a bit of time for, given how few social options existed for me anymore. This is what I came up with:

The Philosopher's Song

Could God know when man was made
That, though with immortal ore inlaid,
When all the truth was finally out,
He was immortal but in doubt?
When the Potter stopped his wheel
To slap on man the celestial seal,
Did He shrink from what He saw?
A crack was there, a mortal flaw
That marred the Potter's visage bright
In what was meant to reflect His light,
In what was perfect else created—
And what had this necessitated?
Why not then annihilate?
Or was it even then too late?
Then must we keep up all the shows,
Although He knows we know He knows?
So we will play out all the play
As if we knew not what to say,
We'll try to believe in all our lies,
Deceived to think we improvise.
But I would know, if know I could,
If, when the final product stood
Before his Maker in naked state,
Was he abandoned to his fate
With all his crimes upon his head
And all the words already said?
Or did the Maker have a change of heart,
Did He take pity on His objet d'art
And decide to give him—us—free will,
Made of clay but still perfectible?
Were we allowed a chance at self-creating?
I'd like to know. I'm here. I'm waiting.

I was proud of that last line, it had surprised me, and I'd never written anything like it before; but I had no one to share it with. I thought for a brief moment of showing it to the vaunted English poet who taught our group. But then I flashed on his besotted face with his hand up a young teacher's business, and it was obvious even to me that this would not be a very smart move. So I put the poem away and returned to my Shakespeare. In fact, I did such a great job of moving on to other concerns that it's only now, forty-plus years later, that I discovered it in my notebook, unseen, unknown, unpublished until now.

The fact is, I moved away from such highly-structured, rhetorical, classically-influenced, rhyming verse after this, and I was probably embarrassed by it. But reading it again now, I'm impressed by the ambition and find merits that I didn't before. (I'm not being self-congratulatory, believe me; I am currently so far removed from the mindset that gave rise to it, that it's more like discovering a poem by somebody else.)

I'll skip over my month in Germany—which was very bizarre, to say the least, as it was only twenty-six years removed from the liberation of Auschwitz, and aging Nazis were everywhere, mumbling "dirty Jew" under their breath (what gave it away? Was it my glasses?)—and go right to my return to the good old US of A. Judging by my notebooks, I seem to have carried the torch for Berman and Cullen throughout my months on the older continent. The pages of my journals are filled with accounts of the paintings I've seen, the classical music concerts I've attended, and the books I have read—books that I knew about because of Berman, books that he would have wanted me to read. Yes, I was still very much the person that Berman and Cullen had made me into, had "slapped their celestial seal" on, and this presented me with a dilemma. I felt a huge temptation to see Berman again, to re-connect with my "Maker," despite all the terrible things that had happened and all the rational reasons not to. But this impulse to call Berman was so strong, I felt like I couldn't control it. What else could I do?

Finally I gave in and dialed his number. He picked up after two rings. I told him that I needed to see him. He said to come by the next day. He also said that he had moved and gave me the address of his new apartment.

Something happened between the time I put down the phone and the time I showed up at his apartment the next day, but I'm not exactly sure what it was. It may be that I read the book Berman wrote about Robert Browning's poem *The Last Duchess* and found it be a boring grad school monograph with nothing original to say. (Which it is; I still have a copy of his book in my possession, and I'm pretty sure that Berman himself gave it to me, but I can't pinpoint when exactly this exchange took place.) Or it may be that all the anger I felt toward Berman finally caught up with me and came to the surface. Whatever it was, by the next day any yearning I'd had for my old relationship with Berman had been replaced by a burning rage that I couldn't wait to express.

I showed up at his new apartment on 72nd Street near the East River when it was still light outside, but it was dark as a cave inside Berman's place. In contrast to the other apartment, this one didn't seem cluttered—at least from the brief glimpse that I got. I saw custom-made bookshelves lining the long hallway on the way to Berman's office—which itself seemed very burrow-like, as if it were some highly-cultured animal's den. Classical music was playing on the turntable (of course), a Bach Fugue. Berman sat in a large chair with a tensor light behind him—it shone off his shaved head and into my eyes.

"You have something you want to tell me, Mr Fife?" he said.

"Yes," I told him. "You're a terrible, destructive person."

"Is that so?"

"You make yourself out to be this great genius, but you're not. You don't really know anything."

"And why did you think this would be of interest to me?"

I had meant to be strong in my anger, but I was already dissolving into tears and losing the thread of what I wanted to say.

"You said you wanted to teach me and make me a better poet, but you didn't teach me anything. And you made me hate poetry," I said, wishing I could come up with something better, something that would really hurt him.

"I think it's time for you to leave, Mr Fife."

"You fooled me for a while, but you're not fooling me any more," I stammered. "You're a deeply deluded person."

Mr Berman had gotten up from his chair and was firmly escorting me back along the long hallway.

"It's time you went on your way."

We were at the front door now.

"I look forward to hearing about your dying from a terrible disease," I said. "I hope that you suffer."

Mr Berman laughed in my face, a cold, cruel, poisonous, hate-filled laugh.

"Ah, but it's you who is going to suffer the terrible fate," he said. "You will join a long list of willful children who lashed out and then couldn't make it on their own. What a shame to waste all that potential."

Suddenly Mr Berman was rattling off a list of twelve names with sardonic glee. Yes, this man of lists was giving me one more, the list of all the young men he'd driven to suicide. None of the names was familiar to me, but somehow that made what he said even more frightening.

"You will be the thirteenth boy, and you will have only yourself to blame. So don't come crying back to me."

And then I was outside the door.

Chapter 12

Why do I always feel like there's something I'm running away from?

— from my 1971 notebooks

WHILE COLUMBIA WAS MY ONLY OPTION FOR COLLEGE, David Burstein had many—but he chose to go to Columbia too, and we shared an off-campus apartment. His presence was steadying at first, but somehow we did not become closer, did not become better friends.

Why? I don't know. There was something eating at him that he wasn't telling me, just as there were many things I wasn't sharing with him. I suppose that must have been too much in the end. We didn't have any classes together and rarely saw each other outside the apartment. Even there, I don't recall us eating together very often.

Columbia had all sorts of required courses, but I decided to delay taking most of these and sign up instead for the subjects I liked. This included taking Poetry with the renowned Kenneth Koch, a wonderful writer who had come of age with Frank O'Hara and John Ashbery, two of my favorite modern poets. Koch was neurotic and charming and brilliant, but I never really connected with him. His concerns often seemed too aesthetic for me. I felt too damaged to be aesthetic. I felt numb and wasn't able to process much of the new experiences that came with being at college. Berman's curse followed me everywhere, a whisper beneath the sounds of the world that I did my best not to hear. I felt a grim defiance, I vowed not to give Mr Berman the satisfaction of giving in to my despair.

ENDURE

I shall endure
as a barnacled rock
that outlives the fragile shore.
With the driftwood found
beneath obscure mounds of dirt
I shall inscribe my name
upon the seasons' golden sand.

Though waves of fury
flog this ebbing shore
until only barren cliffs remain,
the words of mine inscribed here
shall endure.
Even though I walk a lonely path,
my soul shall strive ahead.
The torn heels of my shoes
shall trace upon this black dust
a trail for other men to follow.
I must be known for what I am
not for what I seek to be.
For freedom is what will make us strong
and strength is what will make us free.
And those who falter before the dawn,
who seek to rise but fall back into sleep,
they shall be as a shiny plaster statue
that time's chisel chips away to nothing,
piece by piece.

I was trying to find a way back to the original impulse that made me want to write, that made me love poetry in the first place. Columbia was the intellectual and spiritual home of the Beats, and, while I've never been a huge Kerouac fan, I loved and admired Allen Ginsberg's *Howl*, as much for its wacky beatnik excesses as for its deliriously articulated wisdom. I tried to draw strength from that, even while I was a very different kind of writer.

PHONE

a curse dies
within the throat
as he stares at the phone and
gently places it on the receiver and
weeps with unusual softness over
the fallen bird by the side of the road and
other insignificant details until
he is disgusting, dripping with
self-pity.
the cry is lost
on the lover's lips

as it hits him—
he's lost love, life
has never lived, loved,
never thought—
thoughts revolve in his head but
he dismisses all as
morbid and ridiculous as
he turns off a night light and
a pillow
glides into place.

Mostly I ached for a lover who would understand me and take away some of this pain. My sense of desolation overwhelmed any attempt to make a connection on campus. Then, in a massively foolish move, I began writing to C., the girl from the Oxford course, telling her that I felt we were meant to be together. She was the daughter of a famous professor at Princeton and had confided in me how oppressive his influence had been on her life, how smothered she felt by his over-protectiveness. I wrote to her that I would be coming up to Princeton the day after Thanksgiving to rescue her from her father's house and take her back with me to Manhattan.

Evidently she showed my letter to her father, because when I phoned her from the Princeton train station, her father answered and told me that C. had a message for me. Then C. got on the phone and said that she couldn't see me that evening, but, since I had come all this way, she would meet with me for fifteen minutes at 8:30 AM the following morning. I begged her to meet me away from her father's house, somewhere that we could really talk. There was a momentary hesitation, a catch in her voice, then she stated very firmly, "You have heard my terms. If they are not satisfactory for you, then I'm afraid I won't be able to see you." Then she hung up.

I didn't have much money with me (of course), and I didn't even think about splurging for a motel room. I got a bite to eat at a diner near the station, then I began walking. I ended up at the university campus, which was empty because of the holiday weekend. (Had I applied here? It's possible.) I found an open building and walked in. There was a carpeted room with a few chairs and a table. And most importantly, there was a large clock on the wall so I could keep track of the time. Unfortunately the fluorescent lamps could not be turned off, but at least they gave me some light to read by. I took out a copy I'd brought with me of J.W.N. Sullivan's biography of Beethoven (one of Berman's favorite books—some habits die hard) and started reading. Around 2:30 AM, the hopelessness and absurdity of what I was doing hit me with a jolt.

How did I ever think this could work?

The simple answer was, it couldn't. But I didn't know what else to do.

All I wanted now was to be happy, to find some kind of happiness. I didn't care about genius or talent or anything else, just finding a woman who could return my affection and give me the understanding I wasn't getting anywhere else. But, even in my present state, I understood that desperate moves such as this one rarely resulted in anything good. It's just that I felt so buried in misery, so lost, and I didn't know how to find my way out. I was a walking open wound, I left a blood trail behind me wherever I went. What woman could I hope to find who would freely choose to be part of such an arrangement?

So yes, the meeting with C. occurred the next day, and nothing came of it. We spoke for a few minutes with her father sitting a few feet away, and it was pointless, awful, grotesque. I was exhausted when I got back to upper Manhattan, and not just because I had gotten so little sleep. I felt mentally and spiritually wrung out, more hopeless than ever. I had let much of my schoolwork slide to take this ill-advised romantic foray, and now I had a difficult time concentrating. I managed to write my end-of-term essays, but cramming for finals was useless.

I walked out on all the exams, so I finished my first semester with two A's (Poetry and Humanities) and three incompletes.

My family had a trip planned for winter vacation to a resort in a remote part of Mexico. I had already told them that I didn't want to go. I stayed in their apartment while they were gone, hoping to get my life into some semblance of order. (Also David Burstein was spending the vacation with his family, and I didn't feel like being in our apartment alone.)

Of course, spending time at my parents' place also meant revisiting the room behind the kitchen that was so fraught with dark memories for me. (Even if the darkest memories, the ones of my childhood abuse, lay dormant in my unconscious.) Walking into my parents' bedroom, I couldn't help but vividly recall my lovemaking there with Lisa. Ah Lisa, earth goddess Lisa, how much did I miss you now? And not just the sex—no, that was a small part of her absence. She was perfect for me, so compassionate and understanding, so loving and sweet. If not for Berman, I was sure we would still be together. One more reason to hate him. One of so many.

There were a few times when I was reading in my bedroom and looked up at the clock, and it was 2:30 AM—and I would shudder, feeling like I might as well be back in that Princeton room with the fluorescent lamps for all the sense of "home" that I felt. I was an outsider everywhere, even here where I had grown up, and I had somehow managed to turn everywhere into places I didn't belong. I didn't want to dwell on this, because it could only lead to a deeper depression. But really, could it get any worse?

And then on New Year's Day, the telephone rang—and it did.

My maternal aunt had been up in a rented house in the Hamptons with three of her four children, and there had been a fire. She and her youngest child (and only son) had been killed. Efforts were being made to contact my mom at her resort, where the phone system was very primitive. The funeral would take place as soon as my family returned to the city.

I couldn't hang around in my parents' apartment alone anymore, it just felt too tragic, too strange. So I walked around the city for two days, going to movies, hanging out in restaurants, thinking about my aunt. She was a brilliant and beautiful woman, a psychology professor at New York University. But she also had remarkable patience and was a wonderful listener. She somehow found time to meet with me when I wanted to talk about death, of all things—how I saw it everywhere, how it haunted me. She was always so loving and helpful. And now she was gone. How could such a thing happen?

Eventually my parents and brothers arrived, and the funeral took place.

I was in the limo on the way from the funeral parlor to the cemetery when I got an idea for a poem. It seemed obscene to write at such a moment, and yet what else could I do? The words wouldn't go away until I had written them down.

> *Touch us with noble anger*
> *To cry so the dead may hear*
> *The sorrow that stays with the living*
> *When the dead have no longer to fear*
> *The shriek of a child at midnight*
> *The waiting for her to appear*
> *Who has promised her love. Smite*
> *Us with resolution*
> *To fill the unhallowing air*
> *With cries that resound like thunder*
> *That roar beyond lengths of year*
> *Of a life that is fierce with wonder*
> *And a death that is without fear*
> *Of what lies so far under.*

My aunt and her eight-year-old son were buried in the same casket. The sorrow that everyone felt at the gravesite was so real and so palpable and so communal that for a moment life seemed to go through a sea-change, and I glimpsed a different world, one that was honest, full of meaning and about primary things. For that moment, I felt like I belonged.

Then we all packed back into the limos, drove to my aunt-and-uncle's apartment and ate deli food and sweets, talking about nothing, invoking the God of Superfluous Things to once again commandeer control of our lives.

Then I felt more alien than ever and wanted only to join my aunt and cousin in "some better place."

"That is a horrible thought," I told myself. "You mustn't think it."

I was able to suppress it for a few days, in respect of the genuine grief that everyone was feeling, and the ceremonial behavior that such grief demanded. But once I went back to my apartment near Columbia, that mordant thought returned, except in angrier and more outraged form. I didn't sleep at all for a week except occasional moments when I dreamt behind my eyelids. I couldn't sit in one place for more than ten minutes, so when I attended lectures, I had to sit in the back so I could exit hurriedly when the rage became too great.

I wanted to kill myself so badly that it was the subject of all my fantasies, it seemed more appealing than sex ever had. I had an almost sensual attraction to the idea of death, it was like an appetite, a hunger, that had to be fed.

I thought back on my encounter with actual death at the gravesite and had this new interpretation of what that moment signified in terms of my life.

> *I am a wanderer*
> *in a cemetery,*
> *someone at sunset*
> *who took a pointless walk*
> *among the hills of stone*
> *and thought his name*
> *was whispered in the distance*
> *but was wrong.*

Still, if I really wanted to die, then wouldn't I have been dead already? As disfiguring as my emotional pain felt, and as attractive as death seemed, I've always hated to admit defeat. (And I could never see self-murder as anything but a defeat.) But the screams in my head were getting louder all the time, and I didn't know how much longer I could hold out against them. If I'd had any affinity for hard drugs, then I would surely have gone that route. But I was afraid of losing any further control of my life. For the same reason that I wouldn't submit completely to Berman, I also wouldn't shoot smack.

(Or maybe the innate cautiousness of my forebears was simply asserting itself.)

What ultimately saved me from self-destruction was that my parents had finally agreed to support my wish to see a psychiatrist.

Why? Well, the tragic deaths of my aunt and cousin now provided a "reason" for my needing to see a therapist, a "reason" that hadn't been there before.

Also, my aunt had been close friends with Dr Eugene Goldberg, who was well-regarded in professional circles, and who agreed to take me on as a patient. So, when I disclosed my "family secrets," the person I was disclosing them to wouldn't be a "complete stranger." (Odd as it may seem now, Columbia University did not have free or even inexpensive mental health counseling for students at that time.)

Chapter 13

And I only am escaped alone to tell thee.

—Job, quoted by Melville in the Epilogue of *Moby Dick*

ALL MY READINGS OF FREUD AND JUNG and other practitioners of psychiatry hadn't helped in the least in dealing with the emotional damage inflicted by Berman and by my aunt's death. But just a few sessions with Dr Goldberg proved to be of enormous benefit in relieving the internal pressure I felt to harm myself. He cared—or he certainly seemed to—and that concern for my well-being by a responsible adult who saw and heard me just meant everything. It made me feel like my personal dilemma *mattered*, and that it was a real thing worth taking seriously, not some posture I was putting on in order to get attention. This gave me a lifeline of hope when I needed it most, one that I gladly and eagerly grabbed on to. I hate to think how things would have turned out otherwise.

One thing I realized fairly quickly in my meetings with Dr G was that I could no longer sit in a room by myself and work on my poetry. My sorrow and despair just went too deep, it was more than I could handle in such isolation. I started looking around for other ways to express myself. Performing for the stage had attracted me for a long time—even at Horace Mann, where I envied David Burstein his acting ability, but felt too self-conscious myself—now I saw the benefits of the collaborative nature of that art form, and I started trying to deal with my shyness and channeling my energies in that direction.

All the time I was doing this, of course, I still felt under the weight of Berman's prediction, his parting "curse." Would I indeed become "the thirteenth boy"? Suicide still seemed like an option whenever the pain became too great and the future looked too bleak. Even with the help of a dedicated professional like Dr G, I still had trouble keeping my self-destructive impulses at bay, especially after going through a series of volatile relationships with women, couplings that began with intense passion but soon burned themselves out.

At the bottom of everything, I could still hear that voice in my head whispering, "You'll never get out of this hole. Why not cut your losses and end it now? You had your chance at doing something special with your life, and you blew it. Why stick around any longer? Who will really miss you?"

I can honestly say that at certain times my only answer to these self-loathing thoughts was that I refused to give Mr Berman that satisfaction, I was not going to let him believe that he had succeeded in driving me to take my own life. I was not going to let Berman win. I vowed not to be "the thirteenth boy," no matter what. (Ironically, that curse of his might have been the very thing that kept me alive through my worst episodes.)

It took me another year and a half, but I eventually did the work necessary to remove all my "incompletes" at Columbia, I cleaned up my academic record and even got on the Dean's List. Then, oddly enough, I dropped out—mainly because Columbia had just eliminated their undergraduate theater major.

During the year I was out of school—doing various theater projects and trying to decide what to do with my life—I went to visit my friend Arnold K. from Horace Mann. He was attending a Midwestern Liberal Arts College—a school I was considering transferring my credits to.

I stayed on the floor of Arnold's dorm room for a few evenings while auditing various classes during those days. Arnold seemed to be in a good place, he was handsome as ever with his long light brown hair falling gracefully onto his shoulders and his ready smile; he was popular, with a lovely campus girlfriend and many close friends. I don't remember talking about Berman with him at all. Mostly we spoke about this college, and then about fellow classmates from high school, and what they were up to. I didn't see Arnold in the years that followed (I didn't end up going to his college), but I kept up with his progress through our mutual friend Seth Cooper.

I had heard from Seth how Arnold had been accepted at Harvard graduate studies for Art History—which was somewhat surprising, since that never seemed to be his obsession, and I hadn't known he was even considering it as a career path. But it wasn't nearly as surprising as hearing what happened two years later—when Arnold took his own life, hanging himself in the basement of his parents' suburban home.

All those who knew and loved Arnold were shocked, stunned that this guy who seemed to have everything to live for had snuffed out his life this way, and we searched around for answers. Arnold left no suicide note, but I discovered much later that he had written an essay while at his Midwestern college that spoke eloquently about the forces doing battle for his soul at that time. The essay was written for a Religion class in which each student had to articulate his or her "Life Philosophy." Arnold chose to write about the powerful influence that Mr Cullen and Mr Berman had exerted on his fourteen-year-old self while he was a ninth grader at Horace Mann, an influence that had stayed with him.

Arnold paraphrased Cullen's life-advice as "Live intensely, boys . . . Live creatively and feel things deeply. Avoid the death-in-life ways of your money-grubbing parents. Artists suffer, boys, but oh their joys, oh their joys."

Arnold described his own reaction to this as, "How I longed to be among the budding geniuses whose joy it was to have Cullen guide them!" He chronicles how Cullen "took an interest" in him, counseling him to turn against his parents, telling him how "I was destined to join the unproductive ranks of middle-class Jews unless I made a concerted effort . . . to attain something better." Accordingly, Arnold resolved that "in order not to disappoint [Cullen], I summarily rejected my parents."

But then Arnold's drama went through a shift, as Cullen handed over his tutelage to his "bosom-buddy," Mr Berman, whom Arnold described as "the more powerful of the two . . . a thirty-six-year-old Napoleon [who] set himself up as the Genius on Campus." Arnold described how he was called into Berman's classroom "in the late Spring" of his freshman year and "wooed" with an offer that Berman made him. "Do you wish which of the following three lives, Arnold: a) to leave no monument behind you (e.g. a store owner) b) to leave a quickly-forgotten monument behind you (e.g., like your father) c) to live immortal in a creation (e.g., like John Milton)." [Note: Arnold's father was a renowned immunologist.]

Arnold's response to Berman?

"Being only fourteen and a real jock didn't stop me from recognizing the answer which he hoped me to choose and from giving it with conviction: "There is absolutely no question in my mind, sir. I want to live and create things by which to live immortally." (Exactly what that meant was not clear to me then, nor is it clear to me now.) He said those words I had so longed for him to say, "Good, Arnold, there is hope for you. You are special.""

Berman then invited Arnold to join a three month excursion to Europe, along with ten other students who were already enrolled. Arnold felt he had to go, that this was his "destiny." But his parents weren't so easily convinced. "My parents were well aware of [Berman's] reputation as both a powerful mind and a possible queer [sic]." Arnold told Mr Berman of his parents' reservations about letting him go on the trip. Mr Berman in turn explained to Arnold that his parents were simply "expressing their desire" to "mold me into their sort of mediocrity." For Arnold, "these were fightin' words. I was determined to escape the pressures that their sickness (as outlined by Berman) caused them to impose so relentlessly on me. I won. I went with Him (now deified)."

So Arnold went with Berman and the ten other students to Europe for three months. Arnold described how Berman "used to play ferociously with the jealousy that circulated among us." According to Arnold, Berman would "confide" to him: "Arnold, you are the only one of the boys for whom there is hope. Just look at their envy of you. All great men are desired by their lessers." Arnold named their group "the Bermanettes" and enjoyed recounting how soon all of them sounded like their leader, using "the carefully sculptural, loftily ambiguous sort of sentence-forming which was a trademark of Berman." Arnold wrote that "Berman used to tell us that he was a conglomerate of every great man who had ever lived." But always it came back to Berman's "wooing" of him, with lavish words of praise. "Arnold, you out of all the others have the most vast potential. I have been teaching for many years indeed, but never have I encountered a student whose possibilities were as prominent as yours. If only you will let me, I will guide you . . . Ah, how many great ones I've seen fail . . . You will not be one of those, will you, Arnold? It would kill me to see you, of all the others, not make it. I love you. Please."

But amid all his devotion to Berman—and his gratitude at having been singled out as Berman's "favorite" in the group, Arnold couldn't help noticing how everything with Berman was always, "*The* greatest something or other. Superlatives ran like water. . . . He set himself up as *The* greatest intellect and was generous enough to offer us *The* greatest lists of all *The* greatest things." In addition to Berman's list of *The 1,000 Greatest People Who Ever Lived,* there were also, "The ten finest pianists alive, the ten finest pianists dead, the twenty top museums in the US, the ten top museums of Italy, the thirty greatest novelists who wrote in the nineteenth century, the six greatest newspapers in Austria, etc. etc. ad nauseum . . . It reached the outrageous point that if Mr Berman said, "Boys, this fountain pen is *The* finest model ever conceived by the mind of technology," we would all not only accept this unquestioningly but perhaps even proceed to purchase one." And Arnold confided in his essay that, in the back of his mind, a small voice kept telling him, "There's something wrong. It cannot be correct, what this man is trying to do."

And what was Mr Berman "trying to do" to Arnold? Well, first, he wanted Arnold to shear his beautiful light brown locks. "You need not shave yours [as I do], but you simply cannot continue showing yourself so foolishly," Berman is quoted as having told Arnold. But what else did Berman specifically ask of him? Again, as in my case, it wasn't Arnold's body that Berman was overtly demanding, it was his soul. "Do you or do you not wish me to help you?" Berman demanded, according to Arnold's essay. "Do you or do you not wish me to give you all that I have in order that you become great?"

This presented the fourteen-year-old Arnold with a terrible dilemma, just as it had done for me at a slightly older age. "He was the only adult in my life for three months. I desperately needed to be accepted by an adult figure; I desperately needed to be accepted by him." Also: "How could I, his favorite, reject [him]?" So Arnold tried to make a deal with Berman, he tried to craft a compromise, just like I had done. "O.k., Sir, I will follow almost anything you tell me to do. I do so fervently want to become a genius and I trust you almost totally," Arnold described himself as having said. But Berman wouldn't accept any compromises, saying that it "implies that you want only partially to become a great man . . . Your partial trust in my discretion implies that you place your own above mine. Is that so?"

Arnold continued to plead: "Please do not ask me to sign my soul to you forever. Please, Sir, you scare me terribly." Berman's response—as recorded by Arnold—sent chills of recognition down my spine. "Arnold, you are a fool. Please go away . . . You are no longer a possible Milton, you are a sure Arnold. You are happy with the death that you have chosen, are you not?"

Berman's rejection sent Arnold into a tailspin, again in ways that bore an uncanny resemblance to what I'd been through. "I went berserk in Rome," Arnold wrote. "I went absolutely nuts." Did he sneak into Palatine Hill and lie down in a sarcophagus too? He didn't specify in what ways he went "nuts," but it certainly would have made sense to me if he had.

Arnold recorded that he tried to calm himself down by pouring his heart out to his classmate and best friend on the trip, but this backfired on Arnold.

"Mr Berman has told me of your limitless creativity, but you spit in his face," the friend scolded him. "I would do anything to insure my own immortality and a place in his heart. I think it's really funny, the fact that you are the only one he wants and yet you are the only one stupid enough to reject him." Arnold recounted that his friend "laughed all the way to the Vatican. I cried."

And who was this best friend, identified in Arnold's essay only by his initials? He was another fourteen-year-old boy, the only D.B. on the trip: David Burstein.

(I had never heard this story from David before I read it in Arnold's essay, but David has since confirmed to me that he was indeed the one whom Arnold had confided in on this trip.)

It's important to note that Arnold wrote this essay almost six years after the events he was describing had taken place. His purpose was to declare his freedom from Berman, his break with the past. He concluded by writing, "With this paper I would like to finish the Bermanic period of my life and rededicate myself to that which exists concretely, rather than that which exists in appearance. I will remember Mr Berman not as an abstract force whose affect on me was metaphysical, but as a man, a particular man whose influence led me to reject abstractions in favor of the specific."

Early on in his essay, Arnold described himself as "being counted among the ones who [Berman] tried to 'save' but failed to. I am one of the lucky fish who got away." But did he ever really get away? While Berman's foremost disciple, Robert Simon, made his fortune by applying his master's directives in the Old Master Art business (check out "Robert Simon Fine Art" for confirmation), this was not Arnold's field to pursue. It seems to me—and this is just my opinion—that by doing so, he was trying to beat Berman at his own game. But "special-ness"—much less "genius"—is a rigged contest, at least if you use Berman's rules. It depends on someone else whose opinion you revere declaring that you are special, a genius. It's not a game that you can win with yourself, especially when that self has been damaged so expertly and so profoundly by such a demonic manipulator.

In Arnold's case, even the Harvard imprimatur wasn't enough to counter the private voice whispering in the night that he was a failure, "destined" (as Cullen had warned against) "to join the unproductive ranks of middle-class Jews." Cullen had declared this to be "synonymous with death"—that is, before handing Arnold off to his "bosom-buddy" (to quote again from Arnold's essay). What difference then to kill himself if he was already destined for death? Why stick around and tough it out if the best he could be would never be good enough, if he was simply going to join the ranks of "the walking dead?"

As it happens, Arnold and I were both in Berman's class on John Milton, where we studied *Lycidas*, the great poet's elegy for "a learned friend, unfortunately drowned." These lines from that poem seem to apply:

> *Bitter constraint and sad occasion dear*
> *Compels me to disturb your season due;*
> *For Lycidas is dead, dead ere his prime,*
> *Young Lycidas, and hath not left his peer.*
> *Who would not sing for Lycidas? He knew*
> *Himself to sing and build the lofty rhyme.*
> *He must not float upon his watery bier*
> *Unwept, and welter to the parching wind,*
> *Without the meed of some melodious tear.*

My heart weeps for you, Arnold. You were too hard on yourself, you deserved better. The graces were kind to you, amigo—you had looks, brains, compassion and a quick wit. You had privilege and place and were loved by your family. This world was made for you, Arnold, it should have been yours to enjoy. Instead you ended up as another item on one of Berman's lists. *"Top 13 Boys That Robert J. Berman Has Driven to Suicide."*

Yes, there you are. His "13th Boy."

I'm glad it wasn't me, but it shouldn't have been you either, Arnold.

Now rest in peace, my brother. R.I.P.

Chapter 14
The Ghosts Come Home to Roost

IN LATE 1975—JUST A FEW MONTHS before Arnold took his life—I ran into an acquaintance from the class above mine at Horace Mann who had also been on the staff of *The Manuscript*. He said that Mr Cullen had suddenly quit teaching in April, three weeks before the end of the previous school year, and did I have any idea why?

I told him that this was the first I'd heard of it. He seemed surprised that I wasn't more in the loop, surprised that I wasn't able to shed any light on the matter. But the fact was, I'd simply been going through too many changes myself to stay in touch with anyone, and the Internet—that ideal vehicle for staying in touch—was still more than a quarter of a century away. There were no cell phones either, of course, and very few people even had message machines on their home phones. It was very easy to lose touch with the people you'd known, which sometimes wasn't a bad thing. In fact, sometimes it was what you had intended.

In the two years since I had dropped out of Columbia—and the four years since I'd been in high school—I had performed in a few plays Off-Off Broadway (including at the famed La Mama), and I had been in something like six or seven movies, all independent short films or features by recent graduates of the Columbia or NYU film programs. (For some reason, I always seemed to get cast as the weird but interesting outsider, either angry with a girl who had dumped me or spying on a girl I was attracted to). I had also done a bus & truck tour of east coast colleges with a stage adaptation of Ovid's *Metamorphoses*, in which I played Achelous the River God, who hailed himself as "the world's greatest lover" until Hercules came along and kicked his butt. (The scenery was minimal, as were the costumes. Mine consisted of a macramé top and very brief shorts—really more like a Speedo bathing suit.) Then it was on to Carnegie-Melon University for a year in the Acting Conservatory, which was arduous and exhausting but fun—at least until I got kicked out for "having a New York attitude" (ah, some things never change).

It was all refreshingly different from sitting in a room trying to write masterpieces, but now here I was again, back at my desk, hunched over

an electric typewriter. (No personal computers yet—got that?) I was enrolled at Sarah Lawrence College, where I was taking a Fiction Writing
class with the wonderful Grace Paley. When I heard about Cullen's sudden
departure, I decided to write a piece of speculative fiction about it. Weird,
huh? But all those dark, painful secrets—they were still buried too deeply
for me to touch them. That is, I *had* told a few people about Berman. Dr G,
of course. And Arnold's friend Seth Cooper, I told him about my having
been naked at Berman's (though not about anything else). And I'd had several girlfriends at Carnegie-Melon, I'd told a few of them aspects of what
had gone on. Anyway, my two years hiatus from writing had given me a
sort of Salinger-esque nostalgia for the more conventional aspects of my
high school experience, and that's what I felt safe enough to write about.
(The resulting novella is included in an online appendix. See the copyright
page for the url.)

Some years later, a friend forwarded a copy of a letter to me that Mr
Cullen had sent to *The Horace Mann Record*, in which he made crystal
clear his reasons for quitting so abruptly. Cullen had tendered his resignation as both teacher and English Department Chair to Headmaster Clark
because of a combination of personal health problems and a disappointment in the school's direction, a feeling that its educational standards had
been irreparably lowered. Cullen had agreed to serve out the school year,
and his only parting request was that Mr Berman replace him as head of
the English Department. Clark instead had chosen another English teacher
to be the new Chair (one who had an impeccable record and has never
been tied in any way to the Sex Abuse Scandal).

Cullen was apoplectic. "As I sat in Mr Clark's living room, listening to
him explain his enormous unexplainable, tragic mistake, a great sadness
filled me, and then a great anger, and knowing that my continuance at
the school could only be construed as tacit acquiescence in an intolerable
wrong, I knew too, and with a thrill of horror, that it would be physically
impossible for me to remain on campus for another five minutes, and I so
informed Mr Clark (for whom personally I continue to have the friendliest
feelings)."

Elsewhere in the letter, Mr Cullen wrote: "The objective fact remains
that, in the possession of the attributes I consider most necessary in a first-
rate English Department Chairman—intellectual power, wide learning,
creativity, spiritual depth, personal force and presence, articulateness, and
an absolute dedication to that very quality of excellence alluded to before—Mr Robert Berman made all the rest of us, including emphatically
yours truly, mere beggars."

This was simply mind-boggling for me to read.

I had told Mr Cullen everything—everything!—that had transpired between me and Berman. I told him how Berman had driven me to hate poetry—which I had loved with all my being before!—and how he had me even at that moment on the brink of suicide. I told Cullen in his own living room how Berman had tried to break down my resistance to his sexual advances, how he had kissed me, fondled me, directed me to masturbate for him and eventually had tried to rape me. I thought Mr Cullen had heard my pain and felt some compassion and sorrow for me. But evidently he hadn't, because otherwise how could he consider such a person to be qualified *in any way* to teach young people, much less to be a prime candidate for Head of the Department?

While I hate and despise Mr Berman—and consider him to be a fraud and a coward, quite literally beneath contempt—it has been more difficult for me to extinguish my love and respect for Mr Cullen, whose own passion for poetry and for revealing the truth of the soul had such a profound effect on me. But his continued endorsement of Berman as a teacher of young people really gives me no choice. He was certainly Berman's protector and enabler, and maybe something more.

I found out recently who the would-be lover was who had broken Mr Cullen's heart, way back when I went to see him in my own desperate state. It was my friend David Burstein. Cullen had appointed him to be in charge of *The Manuscript* and then had begged David to sleep with him. David said "no" over and over, but Cullen wouldn't stop. David basically had to back away from being the editor, he told me, unable to tolerate Mr Cullen's constant demands. (This was what he had wanted to tell me when we were seniors, but which he could no more do than I could tell him about Mr Berman.) I'd love to hear Mr Cullen's side of this story, and what his justification might be; but he died of a heart attack in 1983.

As for Mr Berman, he resigned from Horace Mann in 1979—just a year after he would have had to teach his first coed class there. (I would give good money to have been a fly on the wall in those classes!) Berman's own explanation—included in Marc Fisher's article—is that Horace Mann offered him only a part-time contract for the following school year, which would not have been enough money for him to live on. But I have heard from three solid sources that the truth was otherwise. Their account is that Mr Berman made his offer of "immortality" and "special-ness" to a teenage student whose parents were major school donors. The young man's parents found out—two of my three sources say that he told them himself—and the parents went to the Horace Mann headmaster (Inslee Clark) with a very clear message: get rid of Mr Berman or be prepared to have the school "burned to the ground," financially-speaking. Still, Horace Mann allowed Berman to resign "with dignity." There was no mention of sexual abuse allegations or any other "black marks" on his record, to use Dr Gratwick's terminology from my encounter with him several years earlier.

I'm not aware of anything that would have stopped Mr Berman from applying for a teaching position at other schools, nor any way that those schools would have had an awareness of the darker aspects of his teaching history. But he didn't send out any such applications, as far as I know. Instead he made his own personal bid for "immortality," writing his wildly ambitious novel, *Shepherd's Trade*, which was subsequently published by The Pelion Press in 1982, along with an accompanying volume of annotations to the novel and explanations of its "meanings" (also written by Berman) entitled "What It's All About." The cost of the novel plus accompanying volume of annotations: $100. In 1982, that was lots o' money, especially for a new novel by a writer with no reputation.

That was also the last time I heard from Mr Berman directly. Well, okay, not from him exactly, but from one of his followers, Roger Rosen, HM class of 1973, whose father owned the company that was publishing Berman's *magnum opus*. I—along with Berman's other disciples, past and present—received a personalized mailing from Pelion Press. (Mine was sent to my parents' apartment. I was living at that time just 30 blocks uptown on the upper West Side, having graduated from Sarah Lawrence and married the Latina actress whom I'd been living with.)

The one page publicity release began: "Dear Bibliophile: Don't you wish you had been able to purchase the 1926 Pike/Hodgson subscriber's edition of T.E. Lawrence's *Seven Pillars of Wisdom* or had learned from Sylvia Beach about her Shakespeare & Co.'s 1922 publication of Joyce's *Ulysses*? Now you have an even greater opportunity. Pelion Press proudly announces the forthcoming publication of a limited subscriber's edition of a monumental novel by Robert J. Berman, Shepherd's Trade. Set primarily in contemporary New York and London, the reader is also shown "farther galaxies beyond imagining or reasoning or summoning to the soul side . . . ." We meet such extraordinary people as Mikhail Ostorog, Paul Ruckert, Cipriano Lisante, La Donna Serena, and most important that magnificent Phenomenon made in the image of the Pharoah Akhenaton through whom we learn ". . . What boots it with uncessant care / To tend the homely slighted Shepherd's trade . . ."

The release states that the book is being published in a limited, autographed edition of two hundred and fifty copies. "Each edition will be hardbound in gold-stamped Roxite and individually slipcased. The novel is over four hundred pages in length, with more than forty full-color and black-and-white plates illustrating various places, paintings, and people referred to in the story." The "approximate" publication date is announced as Spring 1983. The release letter is signed by "Roger Rosen, Publisher."

Then, at the bottom of the release sent to me, is a note from Roger Rosen himself, written in blue ink: "Mr Berman asked me to include you in this mailing. He thought you would be particularly interested. Look forward to hearing from you. Best, Roger."

At the time I found this both baffling and deeply disturbing. Given that my last encounter with Mr Berman, more than ten years before, had ended with his prediction of my imminent suicide, while I in turn had conveyed my wish that he would keel over from a terminal disease—how did that lead to my being "included" on any list of his current disciples? What about that death struggle would lead Berman to think that I'd be "particularly interested" in hearing any news about him, much less in forking over a hundred bucks for something he wrote? I mean, there's hubris, and then there's just downright insanity. And this mailing/note from Rosen/Berman I definitely put in the latter category.

(I have since reevaluated this mailing and my reaction. The way I look at it now, Berman and Rosen were simply trying to sell books at that inflated and outrageous price, and I could be seen as a likely candidate, even with the bad blood between Berman and me. Or—and this probably goes more to the heart of the issue—Berman's narcissism is so deeply-ingrained, so all-encompassing, that I doubt he remembered anything about our last meeting, I doubt the very notion of "bad blood" ever occurred to him. In his mind, it was "once a follower, always a follower," and perhaps he thought I was still pining for his offer of "salvation." That is, if he actually recalled me at all.)

Needless to say, I didn't buy a copy. My curiosity was such that I probably would have gone up to $30, but a hundred dollars? No thanks. (On second thought, no, the way I felt then, I didn't want any reminders of Berman, I'd already paid too steep a price for that "privilege.") Several years later—at the beginning of the new millennium, in fact—I did eventually come across an HM alum who casually mentioned that he owned a copy. I asked if I could borrow it, and he very graciously allowed me to do so.

By this point I was writing my own first book, a memoir about how working in the theater had helped save my life after the death of my aunt; titled, appropriately enough, *Best Revenge: How the Theatre Saved My Life and Has Been Killing Me Ever Since.* (There was nothing about Berman in the book, as I still wasn't ready, willing, or able to delve into that darkness and make the results public.) I had written for *The New York Times, Village Voice, New Republic, Soho Weekly News, New York Newsday, American Theatre* and many other publications (including some poetry journals). I had received a Federal Writing grant, among other grants. I'd had several plays produced in New York, Hollywood, Israel and many other venues and other countries. I'd also taught in both colleges and high schools, had movie scripts optioned, done freelance gigs of all kinds, whatever I could do (short of ghost-writing) to make my living as a writer. It was hard, risky work, often unfair and frustrating, definitely not for the faint of heart.

I was interested in seeing what someone like Mr Berman could produce. "Great writers are also great readers," he would always say. Then what are great readers? Does great reading make great writing? But most of all, I wanted to see what a perfectionist like Berman thought was great writing—he for whom nothing was ever good enough.

Admittedly, I was not completely unbiased, and it would have taken a lot to impress me. But I was not prepared for how depressingly terrible Berman's work is. I am no fan of the well-made novel, where everything is neatly blocked out, all the characters fulfill their appointed roles in the story's development, and the "satisfying" denouement is utterly predictable. Yet even such a by-the-numbers exercise might be preferable to the noxious, solipsistic and self-indulgent mess that *Shepherd's Trade* turns out to be. What a joke! And not even a funny joke, the kind that the author is in on, that plays with the reader's expectation of what a novel is supposed to be.

It's clear that Berman believed that he was striking gold here, that he was treating the public to a level of sophisticated entertainment that they would not be able to find elsewhere. Wrong! Indecipherable failures like his are produced all the time by no-talents with way too much time on their hands. These no-talents are the kind who sneer at storytellers for being childish and simplistic, they yearn for a novel as complex and fascinating as they believe themselves to be. Except they're not. They're just people who think too much and don't feel enough. And that's what his novel is, a window into the inner workings of a man who has lost his soul and replaced it with a boundless narcissism and a whole lot of references to the work of writers who actually have something to say.

While agreeing that Berman's novel is "incomprehensibly dense," Marc Fisher in the *New Yorker* did find it comprehensible enough to extract a storyline of sorts. "The protagonist, Robert, is a young man, an odd-looking, rigid colossus who harbors a "vast abundance of love." He is violently separated from his parents—his father catches his mother with her lover, brutally kills them both, and then slips away in a car—and in their absence he concludes that "nothing matters." He has an ecstatic encounter with an ancient Greek vase." That frankly sounds a lot more interesting to me than the mess of pottage that I did my best to muddle through.

However, one thing that Berman did succeed in doing was re-igniting my curiosity about him. Who is Robert J. Berman, and where did he come from?

I knew that Robert Simon and another man had purchased a house for Berman, a 6,000+ square foot 19th Century mansion on an acre and a half in Tuxedo Park, a gated community in upstate New York near Poughkeepsie. They installed Berman as their guru and lived in the house with him. Other than that, I didn't know much, and I couldn't find anyone else who did. Not, at least, until Amos Kamil's article came out in the *New York Times*, and the Not Alone group of Horace Mann survivors of sexual abuse had been formed.

Two of the survivors are former disciples of Berman. They were referred to by Marc Fisher in his piece as "Gene" and "the bond trader," and I'll retain those pseudonyms. Both were also represented by Gloria Allred in the action against Horace Mann, and I was able to find out from them what my existence would have been like if I had given Berman the control he wanted over my life.

Mr Berman had taken Gene home with him from Horace Mann to his apartment on East 72nd Street, told Gene to lower his pants and underwear, and then had sodomized him while reciting from Ecclesiastes 4:11: "If two lie together, then they have heat; but how can one be warm alone?"

Gene was only fifteen years old when Berman first penetrated him. He was a virgin, and he told me that he never had any sexual attraction to Berman or to men in general. Nevertheless he continued returning to Berman's apartment at least once a month throughout his senior year, and he allowed Berman to take over the direction of his life, superceding his parents' authority. He followed Berman's orders to go to college at Columbia, at which time he basically moved into Berman's apartment, rarely using his dorm room. One time Berman commanded Gene and a friend to have sex with each other while he watched, which they did.

Gene had dabbled in poetry while at Horace Mann, though he was not a particularly ambitious or highly-regarded poet until Berman got hold of him. (In Fisher's article, the HM English teacher Mr Warren described

Gene as having been "the most buoyant, happy boy.") Berman had taken over control of *The Manuscript* and suddenly Gene was a literary star, having thirteen poems published in his last two years at the school. Berman gave him A's (he'd been a mediocre student before) and spoke about his being "noble" and "a major talent." But when Gene got to Columbia, Berman steered him away from a Poetry Major, instructing Gene instead to major in Medieval and Renaissance Studies. Gene complied in this, as in so many other things, even though he had no particular interest in any of the subjects he was forced to take for this Major.

Why did he go along with Mr Berman's instructions, even when he disagreed so completely, even violently, with them?

Gene flinched when I asked him this question—"because," he told me, "I struggle so much with that issue myself." He couldn't account to himself for why he allowed himself to be influenced to do so many things he found to be disagreeable and disgusting.

"I was confused, conflicted about so many things," he told me. "Mr Berman had such a strong sense of authority, and I thought he really cared about me. I'm deeply embarrassed to think about this now, but he kept saying the kinds of things to me that I wanted to hear at the time."

That is, until his senior year at Columbia, when one day he just left Berman's and never went back, leaving behind all the belongings and books that he still had there. (Years later he tried to retrieve some of the items most precious to him, but Berman would not cooperate.) He went on to get married and have children, though he is divorced now and very much dealing with the emotional fallout from what he now calls his "lost years."

Gene wasn't able to help me much in disentangling the "real Berman" from all his self-mythologizing stories, except to say that Berman would go to New Haven for one week of each year, but he would never talk about it, and Gene had no idea what the purpose of Berman's trip had been.

The Horace Mann alum known only as "the bond trader" in Marc Fisher's article didn't have much insight into Berman's background either. He did confirm for me that he had helped pay for the Tuxedo Park mansion—dubbed "Satis House" by Berman, after the name of Mrs Haversham's mansion in Dickens's *Great Expectations*—and in fact the trader still partly owned the house. He had lived there with Berman and Robert Simon and Edward Leiter for four years. He had first gotten involved with Berman when he was in 11th grade, when he would come to Berman's apartment and engage in various sexual acts with Berman's other disciples. As he told Marc Fisher, "We didn't think of ourselves as gay, and I never was, though I engaged in homosexual activities, obviously." Berman again described these activities to him as "a natural part of the teacher-student relationship." The trader went on to tell Fisher, "We might spend a night [at Berman's] and then go home to our parents, and other kids would come in. [Berman] took great pleasure in stealing kids from the parents he hated."

On this score, there was at least one instance in which Mr Berman disrupted the family of two Horace Mann students. The story of Adam Zachary Newton and his brother was briefly described by Marc Fisher in the *New Yorker*. Adam Newton's father left the family around the time that Adam was starting high school at HM. Shortly after that his older brother took Mr Berman's class and became obsessed by the art that Berman endorsed: Renaissance painting, Bach and Mahler, Browning and Frost, etc. The brother shaved his head and began to dress like Berman. Soon his brother was trying to get Adam to follow his lead. As Marc Fisher wrote, Adam appealed to other teachers at Horace Mann to intervene, but no one would.

Adam Newton told Fisher that Berman could sense which boys to invite into his inner circle, either because their parents were having marital problems or because the boys themselves were struggling at school. According to Newton, "Berman was preternaturally gifted at remolding people at the vulnerable, liminal moment in adolescence. He had this insidious way of making you feel absolutely singular when he was actually doing this to many people."

Adam Newton elaborated to me, "What separates Berman from all the other cases of abuse we've read about is that he violated not just bodies but identities—cruelly and perversely. When it came to the acolytes he actively sought out, he wreaked singular and grotesque damage on impressionable minds and spirits. In Berman's case, I half-suspect [his] dark desires were of a particularly malevolent sort—a kind of revenge fantasy he was allowed to act, screwing with (mostly Jewish) kids' minds beyond just conniving to screw their bodies. And the fact that Berman was also Jewish—in the minority of his peers at HM, I believe—makes him stand out all the more in my eyes now as a grotesque counter-model. . . ."

Adam Zachary Newton went on to become a University professor of Literary Studies, a choice that he told Fisher was "more than ironic— Freud would say uncanny." He explained that he avoids growing close to students "in some priestly way:" "My job is to facilitate vision and hearing, far from Mr Berman's extreme and cartoonish way, his pedagogy of adulation and awe and devotion." He closed by saying, "Mr Berman was probably the worst English teacher I could have chosen for myself at the most vulnerable of moments. And yet without his influence I do not think I would be where I am now."

Adam's explanation—and especially the ambivalent feelings he expressed about Berman, even after all that he and his family had been through—really touched a nerve for me. It summarized very succinctly what I was feeling when my marriage was breaking up in 1993, and my unresolved feelings about Berman and Cullen came flooding back. I wanted so badly to hate Berman then, with a pure and simple hatred. But he had gotten under my skin in a way that I couldn't forget; the memory of that need I'd felt for him strangely haunted me. Yes, sad as it is to admit, the events of that time almost twenty-five years earlier still reverberated in my soul with a hollow sound that followed me around day and night like my own personal demon. I *missed* Berman—or, more accurately, I missed the sense of meaning and significance that he gave to my intellectual life, my development. I felt an irrepressible gratitude to him for opening up the worlds of literature and art to me, regardless of the price I had paid for them. This made me crazy with anger, and I felt like I had to do something that could help me find a way out of this maze (yes, this "maze of madness").

So that led to the idea of writing a novel about my experiences with Cullen and Berman, hoping that such an act would exorcise the demonic shadows these men had left behind, purging them from my soul forever, along with the latent yearning I still felt at times for someone like Berman who cared about me so much that he would tell me what to do with my life. I decided to write a novel rather than a memoir, since that would spare me the shame of being identified with the dreadful things that had actually happened. Also, my mom had recently finished a term as deputy-mayor of New York City (1989-93), and I didn't want to be the cause of a public embarrassment for her.

I returned to Horace Mann to "scout" the physical layout of the school, so I could describe it as accurately as possible in my novel, even though I was going to think up some snappy fictional name for it. The few teachers from my era who remained at the school had nothing to do with Berman or the circumstances of my abuse, so I did not seek them out. However, when I went down to the campus alumnae office to update myself on the whereabouts of some of my former classmates, I was told that Mr Clinton, the former Guidance Counselor, was about to retire, but he was around if I wanted to speak with him. I said yes, absolutely.

In the fifteen or so minutes that it took to set up this meeting, I made some hurried notes about what I wanted to ask him. My notebook from that day has shorthand sentences to prompt me, such as: "HM sexual abuse policy 1970" (that is, HM's siding with the teacher rather than the student in any claim of abuse) and "You will only tarnish yourself" (a quote from Clinton's message as relayed by Dr Lewerth, warning me to drop my complaint against Berman).

I met with Clinton in his office in the alumnae building. He looked in bad shape, much heavier, his face was blotchy, his nose was swollen and very red. He took out a bottle of Dewar's Scotch and poured us two shot-glasses. During our half hour meeting, he re-filled these glasses a few times. I had been friends with Clinton's son Billy, and Clinton was very upset that day because Billy was sending his son to a school other than Horace Mann. In general, he despaired for Billy, whose life had been very difficult, filled with substance abuse problems with drink and drugs.

I told him what I was planning to do—write a novel about HM and Berman—and he urged me not to. "If you love the school even a little bit, don't do it," he said. He admitted that he had received numerous complaints about Berman over the years, and that he (Clinton) now believed these complaints to be true. "But I couldn't believe it at the time," he insisted, "I thought Mr Berman was one of the most brilliant men I'd ever met, and one of the most cultured too. It didn't seem possible that he could have done these things. I felt like the students were lucky to have such a wonderful teacher."

Clinton spoke about how difficult the late Sixties and Seventies were at a school that was all-boys, but where homosexuality was not and could not be acknowledged. "There was a friction in the air, a tension, but we weren't allowed to talk about it, nobody was." Then Clinton took out the yearbook from the year I had graduated and went through my class, page by page, pointing out all the students who were gay. In several instances I took issue with him, not believing that he was correct. In each case, Clinton told me that he had seen or heard something and could not be mistaken. (One of the boys he pointed to was Ethan Cole, my best friend in seventh and eighth grades. "No way," I told him. "No doubt," Clinton replied with a twisted grin.) When he got to the end of this odd "honor roll," he turned the page to show that year's junior class. The President of that class, Mark Wright, was pictured by himself. Clinton pointed to him and said, "Oh, he was a really big homo." He then described an incident he had personally witnessed, in which Mark Wright had been "porking" an underclassmen in the gym, the younger boy "splayed naked over a pommel horse."

I asked Clinton why he hadn't done something about it, why no disciplinary action had been taken. Clinton told me he had tried to, but the underclassman (9th grader) had begged Clinton not to, saying the sex was consensual between students, and he didn't want his parents to find out. So Clinton had held off (he claimed), and nothing was ever said about the matter.

What I didn't realize at the time was that HM had hired Mark Wright to teach at the school seven years *after* this incident. I didn't make this connection until after I'd read Amos Kamil's piece in the *New York Times Magazine,* in which Mark Wright was named as one of the primary abusers. (Wright had shot himself in the head in a Florida condo a few years after being let go by the school.) Clinton's information had obvious benefits for the survivors, especially those who had been abused by the former gym and art teacher.

Two years later (1996) was my twenty-fifth high school reunion. I decided to return for the festivities. I hadn't made much progress on the novel, but I'd written down a lot of notes, and I was just waiting for a spark that would light a fire under the project. I had recently become friendly again with Mitch Bronfman (who was a player in New York City's art world), and I had a new woman in my life, with whom I was very much in love. I felt like it was time to deal with those difficult experiences from the past and put them behind me.

Horace Mann was also going through a transformation, having recently hired its first woman Headmaster, Eileen Mullady. She spoke to the assembled alumnae, saying that this was a new era at the school, an era of openness and change, but she also wanted to hear about the past, and she would welcome meeting anyone who wished to speak with her. She encouraged us to feel free to make an appointment. I did just that.

On Friday May 10, 1996, at 4:30 PM, I went to see Ms Mullady in her office on the school campus. (I still have the appointment book in which I recorded this date and time in ink.) It was the same office where Tek Young Lin had dragged me by the ear and thrown me down on the chair in front of Dr Gratwick a full thirty years before. This time the mood and occasion were quite different, of course. I found Ms Mullady to be an admirable woman, forceful, smart, energetic. She encouraged me again to let her know what my time at HM had been like, and I proceeded to do so in great detail. She was shocked. Both of us cried on and off. She held my hand afterward, saying how sorry she was that I had gone through such an ordeal—then she, like Clinton, begged me not to write my book or say anything about this to anyone else.

"What good could it do?" she said. "All the people involved are dead or no longer associated with the school, and there is no way to go back and make this right. There's nothing that I personally can do, and the Board of Trustees will not want to hear about it. If you care about the school at all—and I can tell that you do—then I hope you'll keep this to yourself." She ended by saying that her door was always open, and that I could come back any time to speak with her again.

After Amos's article came out, however, Ms Mullady (who left HM in 2005 to take over leadership of a high school outside San Francisco) denied that I had ever disclosed any personal details to her about what I had gone through. In fact, she denied that I had ever come to her office at all, or that she had ever met me. The Bronx detectives investigating the abuse claims were very interested to see my date book, which, they agreed, contradicts her.

In any case, she got her wish regarding my story—I never did write that novel, never could find the spark that could transform my notes from a pile of recollections into a cohesive work of fiction. In retrospect, I understand why. The experience was just too particular, too specific, to lend itself to re-imagining. It was still happening for me, and I couldn't really grasp the events until they had died for me, until they had actually receded into the past. So while I had wanted to write a novel to put an end to the power these events still had over me, the truth was that I couldn't write anything effective until these events had lost their power over me. It's like the drunk man who wants to write a story about what it feels like to be drunk, but he can't do so until he is sober.

(I did manage to write the first chapter, though, which is available in an online appendix: www.cunepress.com/ttb).

By this time, anyway, my life was getting way too complicated. A deal with a producer to turn a play of mine into a major motion picture had just fallen apart, depriving me of a large amount of money. Meanwhile my Latina wife—from whom I was separated—refused to give me a divorce, setting off a nasty legal battle. (New York, still in the dark ages, was a fault state with no "irreconcilable differences".) My new girlfriend got pregnant and then had a miscarriage two months later, leading to our breaking up and canceling our plans to go to Los Angeles together. I then went to LA on my own, established residency, then came back to NYC and convinced my girlfriend to come back with me. Less than two years later our daughter was born, and almost a year after that my divorce was finally completed. And so the years rolled on, and Berman and Cullen and the rest of the Horace Mann story faded into the background for me.

And then Amos Kamil's article was published in 2012, and suddenly all those people and events from the past were very much in the present again. And suddenly I wasn't dealing with my past by myself, I was part of a group of survivors of sexual abuse from Horace Mann High School. And then in March of 2013 I was part of a two week mediation between our group (represented by Gloria Allred and her legal team, along with two other teams of attorneys) and Horace Mann. And then I was in front of another team representing Horace Mann School, to whom I was telling the most intimate and painful details of what I had gone through at the hands of Robert J. Berman, English teacher and "Genius on Campus" (as my late friend Arnold had called him). And then that was over too, and the mediation ended, and I said good-bye to all my new sexually-abused friends and went home to LA, where I sat alone in a room and wondered what it had all been about.

I mean, there was money, yes, I had gotten some money, and that was a very good thing, both for my writing and for my daughter. But the amount was disappointing, given what I'd been led to expect. And the process of dealing with the Horace Mann Board of Trustees was, frankly, horrific, to the degree that it still makes me physically ill just thinking about it. They spent an enormous amount of money hiring a publicity firm to protect their image while stiffing us as much as they could get away with.

And after all the blood and tears that have been spilled, all the wounds that have been ripped and re-opened, Horace Mann School still refuses to allow an independent investigation into these crimes, this corruption. They still hide behind the statute of limitations, claiming that they are exempt from having to answer for their actions—or lack of such, in failing to protect us as students. It's enough to make a person lose faith in humanity—not that this person necessarily had all that much faith to begin with.

But here's the happy ending—sort of. In mid-May 2013, just a month and a half after Marc Fisher's article came out in the *New Yorker,* alerting the world to the unpunished crimes of Horace Mann and Mr Berman, it became crystal clear just who this Robert J. Berman really is and where he came from, thanks to a genealogy document compiled by a cousin of Berman's and discovered on the Internet by the tirelessly resourceful Joseph Cumming.

So Berman is not a Holocaust survivor, he was never married with a child, his wife never died in a car crash—in fact *none* of the stories that Berman told about himself turned out to be true, including the one about his having multiple PhDs. (Let me repeat that: ALL OF HIS STORIES WERE LIES.) The fact is, Robert Berman has *no post-graduate degrees* whatsoever—not even the one he claims in his Browning book to have from Columbia. Berman is the middle child of a Jewish plumber from New Haven. His paternal uncle is a plumber, too. Only one member of his immediate family had even graduated from college. He spent his summers as an assistant plumber to his father in New Haven. He taught for one year at a school in Waterbury, Vermont—where reports have recently surfaced of strange goings-on at Berman's apartment there—and then he was hired by Horace Mann School in 1960, remaining at the school for almost twenty years.

I already knew from the statements of Gene and the Bond Trader that Berman was a big fan of the 1970s TV show *Kojak* starring Telly Savalas, and he used to gather his ad-hoc family/sex partners around him in the evening to watch the latest episode while imbibing liquor concoctions he liked to call "woolies" (for the state of mind they would induce). I also was given access to some correspondence of Berman's in which he quotes "the great Tony Soprano"—so much for his vow never to watch television, "even if the Second Coming were being broadcast."

(In his correspondence, Berman enjoys using the tongue-in-cheek perverse humor of Clare Quilty, the pornographer character from Vladimir Nabokov's *Lolita*. At times his tone seems to mimic that of Peter Sellers playing Quilty in Stanley Kubrick's film version of Nabokov's masterpiece. Like Quilty, Berman enjoys his status as a mocking voyeur, someone consciously playing a character who can exploit the emotional susceptibility of others for his own amusement.)

In a separate document, Berman's relative calls his cousin Robert "a fabulist, highly elusive." Others might prefer the words "liar" or "fraud." Yet in the end, I realized, it may matter less who Berman was than what effect he had on so many young men and their subsequent lives.

"When I survey the most intimate circles of my life now," one of his former followers wrote, "I find parents, brothers, various relations, and only the closest of my close friends. Freakishly, however, somehow Berman also feels written onto my DNA."

That in the end may be Robert J. Berman's greatest accomplishment, his only real "genius"—for creating a character who never actually existed except in the minds of those students he got closest to, who could never really manage to forget him completely, no matter how hard they tried.

Epilogue

There is no pleasure in eating or drinking unless it is preceded by the discomfort of being hungry or thirsty.

— St. Augustine

Amos Kamil's article on Horace Mann's *Prep School Predators* was published in the *New York Times Magazine* on the same weekend as my daughter's bas-mitzvah took place on the west coast.

I first heard about the piece from my friend Seth Cooper and from my mom, both of whom had read it in online when it was posted mid-week. Seth had been the first person other than my shrink who I'd told about my ordeal with Berman, way back when we were students at Columbia in 1973. My mom was shocked that anything so scandalous about the school that three of her sons had attended was appearing in the *New York Times* (which for her, as for so many others, is pretty much as close to "God's Truth" as one can get). I had never told my mom anything about what I'd gone through with Berman, but now it felt like I had to, especially when she kept asking me if I had any idea that such terrible things had been going on while I was at the school. (Neither of my younger brothers who went to HM had a clue that this dark sub-culture existed.) My mom was flying out for my daughter's bas-mitzvah—so how could I continue to keep this a secret? But by the same token, wouldn't it spoil the occasion of my daughter's celebration to bring this up now?

In the end I did tell my mom, but I waited until after my daughter's special day. My mom and I were walking on the Venice boardwalk when I told her there was something we needed to talk about. She heard the seriousness of my tone and looked at me with great concern, worried that I might have a life-threatening disease like the one that had killed my dad. I assured her that this had to do with the article about HM that had just been published. Her expression changed from concern to confusion.

"So you knew about Mr Somary?" she asked.

"No, but it doesn't really surprise me," I replied.

There had been nothing in the *New York Times* piece about Mr Berman—something I'll get back to shortly—so there was no groundwork already laid to make this any easier. There was nothing to do except to dive right in.

"This has to do with Mr Berman, and some things that I went through with him."

"What kind of things?" she asked.

It was another bright sunny day in the southland, people strolled or bicycled past, all around us was abuzz with talk and motion—but I could see a shadow pass over my mom's visage, and everything seemed to freeze in place as I started to describe Berman's seduction of me, his invasive and unwanted kiss, the fruitless complaint I lodged with HM, Berman's attempt to get me to stay with him that summer, and then the visits to his apartment during my senior year and the various ways he tried to break me down.

"You should have told me," she murmured in a small voice from the midst of her shock. "You should have told me what was going on."

"Mom, if I could have told you what was going on then I would have," I said.

This was true in theory—but the opposite was probably even truer. That is, if I could have told her what was going on, then it wouldn't have happened in the first place. The fact was, Berman had wedged himself into the rift between me and my parents. He was a disease, an infection, and this had been his way into my bloodstream. Once there, he behaved like the human virus he was, trying to do as much damage as possible, to destroy my sense of self and co-opt my identity. Not just me, though—this was his modus operandi with all his victims. I was just one of the lucky ones, one of those who survived.

"You fought back, you resisted him—good," my mom said, grasping onto one of the few pieces of good news she could find amid these tawdry revelations.

In truth, this would have been a much harder story for me to tell if I hadn't resisted, if I had given into his demands or had simply been physically overpowered by him. I've seen the kind of psychological damage this has inflicted on his former disciple Gene.

"How could I have let him have such complete power over me for all those years?" Gene has lamented to me. He says that his sense of self still feels tenuous after all these years and after all his accomplishments, both professional and personal (he has several children). In his darker moments, nothing feels real about his life except Berman, and there is nothing about that he feels proud of. He says that he envies my story, with its heroic tilt of not just having resisted but having returned to Berman's place and told him to his face what a despicable person he is. "This is so much harder for me to deal with because I didn't do something like that when I had the chance," he tells me.

I tell Gene in turn that we were simply in a very different place when

Berman got his fangs into us. He was a virgin, I wasn't. He wasn't sure what he wanted to do with his life, while I was already writing and felt certain that this was my destiny. In fact, I was making a Faustian bargain, with Berman as my Mephistopheles, promising that he could give me the world. Gene was simply looking for a sense of direction, for a parental figure who cared more than his actual parents seemed to, and this made him more vulnerable than I was, more pliable, more easily influenced. (One thing that Gene and I had in common—we were both molested as kids. This undoubtedly had a huge effect on our psyches and made us targets for Berman, who had an instinct for wounded souls.)

In the end, my mom listened all afternoon to my account of these long ago tribulations, and she took in as much as she could. She took some comfort in the fact that she had called Horace Mann and complained about Mr Berman's "cult-like" influence over students, though somehow HM's dismissal of her concerns did not make her as angry at the school now as I felt that it should. For the rest, she would interject every now and then, "Oh my, how terrible" or "You really should have said something to me," until I had brought the recounting up to the present. Then she sighed and nodded and said, "Well, you've given me a lot to think about. Let me have some time to process it, and then we'll talk about this again."

While I didn't speak about these events to my mom until after the bas-mitzvah, there were others at my daughter's party who I did discuss them with. One of these was my friend and sometime screenwriting-partner, Ralph Pezzullo. By chance Ralph's wife, Jessie, had also attended Horace Mann, in the class behind Amos Kamil's. She asked me if I had any idea that these terrible events were happening while I was at the school. I told her that I absolutely did, since I was one of the people they happened to.

This led to my giving a brief synopsis to Ralph and his wife of how Berman had derailed my life and almost driven me to suicide, while HM tried to bury the truth. Ralph, outraged, urged me to come forward and tell my story.

"Really?" I said. "You really think I should go public with all this?"

"Absolutely," he said. "You can't let the school get away with this. I don't see that you have any choice."

But I did have a choice, and I wasn't sure that this was something I wanted to be identified with. I'd worked so hard as a writer for so many years, writing poems, essays, articles, plays and films, along with all kinds of freelance writing gigs. I wasn't a household name, but how many writers were? I wasn't making as much money as I would have liked, but again, how many writers were? That was my destiny, where my heart and soul were. That was what I wanted to be known for, writing—not being victim-ized by a warped high school teacher. To be honest, I was more ashamed of falling for this man's flattery and having gone so far down the road to hell with him, than I was of having jerked off in his apartment or anything else. And then there was my daughter—did I want to subject her to the public disclosure of this kind of information about her dad? Not to mention the nieces and nephews of mine who were still attending the school.

The more I thought about it, the less I liked the idea.

But then Seth Cooper told me about the new website set up on Facebook for graduates of Horace Mann to vent their feelings about what had hap-pened back in the day and what was happening now. And then I went on the website and read the posts of former students (most of whom I didn't know) baring their souls, while others ridiculed them or made vicious comments about how students who were "stupid enough" to have sex with teachers were "getting what they deserved." And before I knew it, I was posting about what happened to me and daring anyone to come after me and defending those who had been brave enough to tell the truth, no matter the consequences.

And then that was it, I was out there.

Soon I was contacted by one of the survivors, who asked a few ques-tions about what I'd been through. And when he was satisfied with the veracity of my account, he asked me to join the group that the survivors were forming. And how could I say no to that, after all the years I'd spent trying to get Horace Mann to acknowledge what had happened to me during my years there?

One of the consequences of making that commitment was realizing how angry I was that Mr Berman was still getting away with what he'd done to me, to Arnold K.—and to so many others, as I was now finding out. It infuriated me that Berman wasn't named in Amos's article, and I de-cided to do something about it. I decided to write my own magazine piece, disclosing what I knew about Berman and how the school had chosen to handle my situation. The way I was feeling, it was either write about what had happened or go to Tuxedo Park and put a bullet in Berman's head. As much as the latter appealed to me in a visceral sense, I don't like guns, I don't believe that violence is the answer, and I didn't think this would be setting a good example for my daughter. (Also—I love being a dad and didn't relish watching my daughter's future from behind bars.)

The problem was, it had been years since I'd written journalism, I no longer had any contacts with editors who might assign me the story, and I didn't have enough perspective to edit myself. The memories just overwhelmed me, I couldn't get a handle on the material and didn't know where to start. Worst of all, I had Mr Berman's voice in my head again, telling me, "You're doomed to failure, Mr Fife. Why even try?"

As a last resort, I contacted a friend of my mom's who is a writer for a major glossy magazine, and—after some initial hesitation—she agreed to assist as best she could. With her help—and after many drafts—I was able to craft a seven page magazine version of my story. It wasn't great, and I didn't feel comfortable just putting everything out there so nakedly, but to hell with it—this was the best I could do. Whatever else happened, it felt good to take control of my narrative and be the author of my own story, no matter how terrifying the events themselves still seemed.

I emailed Ariel Kaminer, the editor from the *New York Times Magazine* who had championed Amos Kamil's story (and who had attended Horace Mann), and I sent her a copy of my article with the following cover letter:

Subject: Re: FW: follow-up to your Horace Mann story—regarding the teacher Robert J. Berman

On Thu, Jun 28, 2012 at 2:40 AM, Stephen Fife [email address redacted] wrote:

Dear Ariel,

Here's a personal memoir of what I experienced with this particular teacher, and what I tried to do about it. I am able to provide some corroboration, but obviously private events were private. I understand you have already spoken with Gene, who went through his own version of hell with this same teacher.

I gather from what I heard through the HM survivors' group that you are under the gun to find new news and keep this story alive. I understand how that goes—I wrote a few pieces for the New York Times *"Arts & Leisure" section back in the mid-late 1980s, as well as for the* Village Voice, *and other publications.*

I know that many people hate the school and want to see terrible things happen to it. I don't. It's a wonderful place in many respects. Nevertheless, there were some terrible things going on during my years there, and many smart students were not sufficiently safeguarded by the school. That does make me angry. And I don't feel like I've gotten any persuasive answers yet as to why this was allowed to occur.

I settled in for a nerve-wracking wait—it generally took some time to get a response from an editor one didn't know.

Instead, the response came (shockingly) later that same day.

Date: Thu, 28 Jun 2012 09:55:48 -0400
Subject: Re: FW: follow-up to your Horace Mann story—regarding the teacher Robert J. Berman
From: ariel kaminer [email address redacted]
To: stephen fife [email address redacted]

This is the most mind-boggling document I have ever read. I need to sit in a quiet room breathing into a paper bag. As soon as I manage to screw my head back onto my body I will call you. A.

Wow.

I mean—wow, I didn't expect that.

I mean, editors for the *New York Times* in my experience (and I'd worked with a few) never made statements like that. Editors for the *New York Times* were cautious by nature, cautious and critical—but not given to expressing their feelings, especially not in such human terms.

This was real then. This was happening. My personal narrative was going to appear in the publication that my mom and her friends read like a secular bible, worshipping every Sunday with their bagels and lox. The truth was finally going to get out there, the truth about this teacher and this school and the wrongs that were done forty years ago and were continuing to be done. And people were going to read about it in my own words. Because an editor wouldn't write a note like that unless this was definitely going to happen, right?

Wrong.

Date: Thu, 5 Jul 2012 14:40:40 -0400
Subject: Re: follow-up to your Horace Mann story—regarding the teacher Robert J. Berman
From: ariel kaminer [email address redacted]
To: stephen fife [email address redacted]

Hi Steve—

I'm writing to let you know that the Times *has decided—at a level far above my pay grade—not to pursue a big investigative story into Berman. The sense here is that the paper has already gone to great lengths to establish that in past years, Horace Mann had a major problem with sexual abuse of students by teachers. If there are any news developments—if Berman were for some reason to be arrested, for example—we would definitely consider a news story. But a big free-standing investigation into his past is not, I'm afraid, in the cards.*

I was hoping for a different verdict, but I understand how this one was reached, and I do stand by it. . . . I'm sure you'll have no problem interesting another venue in the story, and I will read (or watch) with great interest when it appears.

Until then, thank you again. A.

Hmm.

I went back to my friends in the HM survivors' group and gave them the disheartening news. There was speculation about what was really behind this rejection, much of it centering around the fact that the *New York Times* had no problem naming three dead teachers as pedophiles, but they might not be so brave when it came to a living one who could sue them for libel, especially one who had become as wealthy as Berman.

(Recently, in the course of granting her consent for her emails to be reprinted here, Ms Kaminer informed me that she never considered using my article as anything but source material for a possible investigative piece about Mr Berman.)

Yes, Berman had become wealthy, largely through his association with his live-in cohort (and former student) Robert Simon's art business. Just two years before this, in 2010—in a story widely-reported around the globe—Simon and another art history scholar had discovered a lost Leonardo da Vinci canvas, *Salvator Mundi*, concealed under a crude copy of the same painting. The former "Clone" was one of a consortium of dealers who had acquired the work, whose worth was originally estimated at a quarter of a billion dollars. (It was subsequently sold to an anonymous collector for around $80 million. Ah, ain't life grand?)

Whatever the reason, that avenue was closed, so I had no choice but to move on. I contacted an editor I knew slightly at the *New Yorker* and pitched it to her. She declined politely, saying that the subject matter was "important" but there was no way in the world that her magazine would be interested in a story that would be seen as an extension or continuation of one that had already appeared in the *New York Times*. I argued that my story was completely separate because it was written by a survivor in his own words—perfect for the Personal Memoir category that was a regular feature of "her magazine." "Sorry," she explained with some impatience, "but the prior association with the *Times* simply makes it impossible."

After much gnashing of teeth I moved on again, sending out increasingly-desperate feelers to other magazines. Then the word came down to me from Joseph Cumming, spiritual leader of the survivors' group, that another writer had emerged, a Horace Mann alum, who wanted to write about what Robert Berman had done. Not only that but this writer had managed to get the story assigned to him by a major magazine.

Which one?

The *New Yorker.* Of course.

And so it was that I became a character in the story penned by Marc Fisher—one of only two "victims" who chose to be identified by name— and it was probably all to the good. Marc is an excellent writer with great personal integrity, and he brought a perspective and understanding to the task that I would never have been able to.

And it propelled me instead to write this book as my way of taking control of my narrative, to whatever degree I was (and am) able to. So there you go then—a happy ending. Sort of. I guess.

But no—I am happy now, happier than I've ever been at least, happier than I can ever remember.

The experience of these last two years has been turbulent and very strange, to say the least. Reliving those nightmarish scenes with Mr Berman in various public forums has been gruesomely difficult and yet oddly liberating. The secrets are out there now, gone, I don't have to bury them anymore or protect myself from their possible disclosure. Unlike most well-educated people in the world, I don't have any reputation to lose, no job that I may be fired from, no associates who I fear may look down on me now. The only person whose opinion of me really matters (besides my own) is my daughter, and she doesn't want any part of this—doesn't want to know my secrets, doesn't want to be distracted from her own teenage experiences or pursuing her own destiny. To which I say, fine, go for it. I will certainly try to protect her in any way I can from stumbling into the same pitfalls that almost consumed me, but there's only so much I can do. I understand that now, better than ever.

I also understand myself and the media and the way the world works much better than I did before. It's a tangled web we've woven, very tangled, and it's hard to see how we're going to come out of it in good shape, but what can any of us really do except try our best to make it better?

And in the meanwhile, life is beautiful, time is short and joy is fleeting. Happiness may be illusory, but it's a hell-of-a-lot better than staring down a dark tunnel into the depths of despair. Trust me—I've been there.

Resources

How to Protect Your Child

(a) Could you Pick a Pedophile out of a Lineup?

In his brilliant and disturbing essay about Jerry Sandusky and "how molesters get away with it," Malcolm Gladwell wrote in a 2012 issue of the *New Yorker*:

When monsters roam free, we assume that people in positions of authority ought to be able to catch them if only they did their jobs. But that might be wishful thinking. A pedophile . . . is someone adept not just at preying on children but at confusing, deceiving, and charming the adults responsible for those children.

Gladwell elaborated on this later: "The pedophile is often imagined as the disheveled old man baldly offering candy to preschoolers. But the truth is that most of the time, we have no clue what we are dealing with." After stating that "pedophiles cluster in professions that give them access to vulnerable children—teaching, the clergy, medicine," Gladwell described one particular pedophile as being "in the business of being likable."

While this was certainly true of Sandusky—the retired Penn State coach, who used the persona of "lovable knucklehead" to help lure in young victims—it didn't apply at all to Mr Berman. Berman cultivated a persona of menace and mystique, and he didn't seem to care about anyone's opinion—about him or anything else. Contemporary psychology (and numerous TV shows) have made us wise in the ways of deception, and how things are usually not what they seem. Certainly someone who looked and behaved as much like a pedophile as Berman couldn't also be one? But he was, and he took great pleasure in driving a wedge between "vulnerable" students and their parents, insinuating himself into the hearts and minds of students until he fully replaced the parents as their authority figure. (The level of contempt in his voice when he spoke about the *nouveau riche* and *bourgeois* parents of Horace Mann kids is something I will never forget.)

But just like Jerry Sandusky, Mr Berman could be charmingly persuasive when he needed to be. This was the case with Arnold K.'s father, a brilliant man in his own right, who opposed Arnold's going away with Berman to Europe for the summer. Arnold's dad demanded a meeting with

Berman. Berman acquiesced, and at the end of the meeting, Dr K.'s suspicions had turned to admiration. "So what if Berman was a bit eccentric?" Dr K said. "He knew so much, and he was steeped in the traditions of world culture; wasn't it wonderful how much Arnold could learn from him?"

And if a brilliant man like Dr K.—a "genius," as many called him—couldn't see through this pedophile's façade, what chance did regular people have?

The fact is, there is no surefire way to see through anyone's façade, no matter what kind of predator or con man they may be. And things are so much more dangerous now than they were in my day, with the Internet and social media providing so many more opportunities for people with bad intentions to make a move on kids or teens.

So what can you do?

(b) Five Ways You Can Help Protect Your Child

1. Have an ongoing dialogue with your child.

2. Respect your child's boundaries.

3. Give serious weight to what your child tells you.

4. Have a genuine interest (and express it!) in who your child is, quite apart from who you might want him or her to be.

5. Do all you can to keep fostering a relationship of trust with your child.

First, a caveat: I am not a psychologist, a social worker or even a teacher (though I have taught my share of writing classes in the past). I am simply an author who was abused as a child and abused again as a teenager, and who has the knowledge gained from those painful experiences. I am also the dad of a fifteen-year-old daughter who lives most of the time with her mom. As much as I love her, I long ago had to come to terms with the facts that I can't protect her to the degree that I'd like, and that I don't have a lot of influence in the parental arena, but I care as much as ever, and I do what I can.

Second, please note that I did not include as one of my five recommendations to "monitor your child's Internet and social media history." This does not mean that I'm against doing so if necessary, or that I don't recognize the necessity of doing so sometimes. I personally feel very uncomfortable crossing that boundary, and it's very hard for me to reconcile that act with the idea of "fostering trust with your child." Again, I personally have never monitored my daughter's computer or scrounged around in her sock drawer, and I don't think that I could look my daughter in the eye if I did. But I know that her mom has checked out our daughter's computer (with her knowledge), and this has not seemed to affect the degree of trust between them. So I suppose it's just a reality of the parent-child relationship these days that a child can't have access to the Internet and social media without allowing full disclosure to the parent, though I can also see the potential this has for irreparably tearing the fabric of the parent-child bond.

And this is the key point for me, that bond—that bond of trust, built on a foundation of patience, love and understanding. That means parents should try not to say things like, "You're just a kid, what do you know?" or "You're living under my roof, and I can go into your room any time I want to," or "I don't care what you want, you'll do what I'll tell you to." Boundaries are so important—personal boundaries in which the child's self can grow—and even a casual violation can have lasting consequences.

That was certainly the case for me with my parents, and it provided ample opportunity for a disease named Robert J. Berman to enter my bloodstream.

(c) How Can I tell When There's Something Wrong with my Child?

Gl adwell wrote in his essay that, "The child molester's key strategy is one of escalation, desensitizing the target with an ever-expanding touch."

My fellow survivor Joseph Cumming put it this way in a recent conversation we had: "If you put a frog into a pot of boiling water, then he will jump right out. But if you put him into a pot of cold water, then he'll swim around, and he won't even notice that the water is getting hotter until he's been cooked."

But how does the predator-teacher decide which "frog" to "cook"?

Gladwell again: "The successful pedophile does not select his targets arbitrarily. He culls them from a larger pool, testing and probing until he finds the most vulnerable . . . "

The "most vulnerable" kids are the ones with a broken or a non-existent bond with their parents or guardians, who have no one protecting them or monitoring their emotional development. That was the case with all thirty-four of the Horace Mann survivors, and that's no coincidence, believe me. We weren't the only vulnerable teens at the school, of course, just the ones who were in the wrong place at the wrong time—or the right place at the right time, as far the predators were concerned.

In the course of my story, I chronicled some of the continuing symptoms of the emotional damage being done to me:

- sleeplessness
- drastic fluctuations in weight
- increasing alienation
- rude and anti-social behavior
- losing one's sense of humor
- mumbling to oneself
- not looking others in the eye
- loss of self-confidence
- disinterest in the future

I've seen these symptoms applied to others who have suffered abuse, though I have also seen abused individuals described as sleeping excessively, becoming unduly argumentative, cutting themselves and other acts of self-mutilation.

Then again, such symptoms can also be applied to other conditions, such as bi-polar disorder or schizophrenia, so it's important to make sure that the young person who exhibits such behavior is convinced to seek help from a licensed mental health professional, who is the only one capable of delivering a diagnosis or offering a way back from the personal and private hell that so many kids have found themselves relegated to.

In closing, stay vigilant. As Malcolm Gladwell warns: "Those who put all their ingenuity and energy into fooling us usually succeed."

Bibliography

Books and Articles on Abuse

Books

Ainscough, Carolyn and Toon, Kay. Surviving Childhood Sexual Abuse: Practical Self-help for Adults who were Sexually Abused as Children. Da Capo Press 2000.

Bass, Ellen and Thornton, Louise, Editors. *I Never Told Anyone: Writings by Women Survivors of Child Sexual Abuse.* Harper & Row, 1983.

Clancy, Susan A. *The Trauma Myth: The Truth about the Sexual Abuse of Children—and its Aftermath.* Basic Books, NYC, 2009.

Copeland, Mary Ellen. Healing the Trauma of Abuse: A Women's Workbook. New Harbinger Publications 2000.

Fleming, Patrick; Lauber-Fleming, Sue; Matousek, Mark. *Broken Trust: Stories of Pain, Hope, and Healing from Clerical Abuse Survivors and Abusers.* Crossroad Publishing, NYC, 2007.

Freyd, Jennifer J. *Betrayal Trauma: The Logic of Forgetting Child Abuse.* Harvard University Press, 1998.

Freyd, Jennifer J. and Birrell, Pamela. *Blind to Betrayal: Why We Fool Ourselves We Aren't Being Fooled.* John Wiley and Son, Hoboken, NJ, 2013.

Gartner, Richard. *Beyond Betrayal: Taking Charge of Your Life after Boyhood Sexual Abuse.* Wiley 2005.

Hamilton, Marci A. *Justice Denied: What America Must Do to Protect Its Children.* Cambridge University Press 2012.

Hunter, Mic. *Abused Boys: The Neglected Victims of Sexual Abuse.* Ballantine Books 1991.

Lew, Mike. *Victims No Longer: The Classic Guide for Men Recovering from Sexual Abuse.* Harper Perennial 2004.

Michener, Anna J. *Becoming Anna: The Autobiography of a Sixteen Year Old.* University of Chicago Press, Chicago, 1998.

Miller, Alice. (trans. by Andrew Jenkins) *The Body Never Lies: The Lingering Effects of Cruel Parenting.* W.W. Norton, NYC, 2005.

Miller, Alice. (trans. by Andrew Jenkins) *The Drama of the Gifted Child: The Search for the True Self.* Original pub. 1982; revised edition Basic Books, NYC 2008.

Monteleone, James. *A Parent's and Teacher's Handbook on Identifying and Preventing Child Abuse.* G.W. Medical Publishing, 1998.

Prendergast, William. *Sexual Abuse of Children and Adolescents: A Preventive Guide for Parents, Teachers and Counselors.* Continuum Publishing, 1996.

Phillips, Donald T. *Unto Us a Child: Abuse and Deception in the Catholic Church.* Tapestry Press, Irving, TX, 2002.

Smedes, Lewis B. *Forgive and Forget: Healing the Hurts We Don't Deserve.* HarperOne Plus, 1996; 2nd Edition 2007.

Theodore, Wayne. *Wayne: An Abused Child's Story of Courage, Survival, and Hope.* Harbor Press, Gig Harbor, WA, 2003.

Articles

Fisher, Marc. "The Master: A Charismatic Teacher Enthralled His Students. Was He Abusing Them?" The *New Yorker,* April 1, 2013.

Gladwell, Malcolm. "In Plain View: How Child Molesters Get Away With It." The *New Yorker,* September 24, 2012.

Kamil, Amos. "Prep School Predators: the Horace Mann School's Secret History of Sexual Abuse." *The New York Times Magazine,* June 10, 2012.

A more detailed list of websites, articles, and books provided by Peter Brooks is available online: www.cunepress.com/ttb

Acknowledgements

THANKS TO THE HORACE MANN ACTION COALITION (HMAC) for their tireless efforts on behalf of truth and justice, especially Rob Boynton, Josh Mannheimer, Peter Brooks, Rob Hollander, Peter Greer and Christina Propst.

Thanks also to my fellow members of the HM "Not Alone" Survivors Group—if there was ever a group I didn't want to be part of, you are it. Yet your camaraderie and solidarity has meant so much to me.

Thanks also to my girlfriend Carolyn K. for her emotional support this past year. And to my daughter, whose presence gives me the strength to bear anything.

A special nod of gratitude to Peter Brooks for allowing me to publish on-line his extensive list of articles that chronicle the HM Scandal and Sex Abuse in general. See the copyright page for a complete list of additional resources or go to: www.cunepress.com/ttb

Index

All the art museums in Europe, 19, 50-51, 81, 88, 100, 102, 117, 158, 182, 188

An American poet at Oxford, 143-146

Brainwashing and mental breakdowns, 157

Childhood experience of molestation, 17-18

From politics to poetry, 12, 14, 16, 27

Genius makes its own rules, 57-58

Going to teacher's apartment, 55, 86, 91, 93, 102, 148-9

Horace Mann Scandal, 1-2, 80-81, 83-84, 165, 170, 175, 177, 182-183, 185-186, 190, 192, 194

How to change the world, 56-57, 89-90, 111

I see your destiny, 16, 49, 114, 150

Isolating me from my friends, 33, 95

Jewish guys going to chapel service, 13, 23

Love hurts, and that's no lie, 67, 153

Mom is a New York politician, 16, 82

Our band of literary brothers, 32-33, 40, 64, 74, 175

Prep School academic pressure, 120

Reporting the pedophile, 68-70, 73, 80, 174

Single sex schools, 16, 21, 129, 132, 134-135, 137, 139-141

The cult-like teachers, 25, 33-34, 37-38, 44-51, 56-57, 59, 61-63, 69-70, 73-75, 77, 80-83, 87-92, 97, 99-100, 102, 104-107, 111-113, 115-119, 121, 123-124, 126-127, 132-133, 135, 138, 141-142, 148-150, 158-162, 165-174, 177, 179, 181-183, 185-186, 188

The Horace Mann Action Coalition, 79-80, 82, 84, 102, 164, 194

The School for Suicide, 31, 51, 86, 134, 158, 161, 163, 185

The school tried to bury the scandal, 36, 81, 170, 176-177

The world outside was burning, 16-17, 59, 87, 138

The world's worst genius pianist, 106-108, 116

Uncovering the truth about teacher, 2, 21, 25, 43, 47, 81-82, 164, 177, 186, 189-190

Upper West Side Jewish home life, 13-14, 17, 19-22, 28, 39, 42-43, 64, 66, 68, 71, 76, 82, 88, 94, 102, 110, 128, 154, 178-179

When Christ appeared to me in Florence, 13, 111

With his tongue down my throat, 39, 62-63, 133, 172, 189

Young love in the late Sixties, 30-31, 34

STEPHEN FIFE's previous memoir, *Best Revenge: How the Theater Saved My Life and Has Been Killing Me Ever Since,* was published by Cune Press in 2005. Cune is also bringing out two books of his poetry, *Dreaming in the Maze of Love-Grief-Madness* and *U & Me & The City.* His plays *Break of Day, Savage World* and *This Is Not What I Ordered* have all been published by Samuel French. Other plays include *Blue Kiss, Sizzle Sizzle, Mickey's Home, Scattered Blossoms,* and *The American Wife* (co-written with Ralph Pezzullo). He also adapted Sholem Asch's play *God of Vengeance,* which has been performed Off-Broadway and in theaters around the US and in other countries.

Stephen Fife also writes screenplays, including adaptations of his plays *Blue Kiss* and *Sizzle Sizzle.* His original screenplay *The Falling Man* has won several awards. He has written feature articles for the *New York Times, New Republic, Village Voice, New York Newsday, American Theatre,* and others. He has edited several books of monologues and scenes for Applause Books. Steve is a graduate of Sarah Lawrence College and Columbia's School of the Arts.

For more: www.stealfireproductions.com. (Photo by Dan Winters.)